Reaching the Wounded Student

Joe Hendershott

EYE ON EDUCATION
6 DEPOT WAY WEST, SUITE 106
LARCHMONT, NY 10538
(914) 833–0551
(914) 833–0761 fax
www.eyeoneducation.com

Hendershott, Joe.
    Reaching the wounded student / by Joe Hendershott.
        p. cm.
    ISBN 978-1-59667-097-6
    1. Underachievers—United States. 2. School failure—United States—
Prevention. 3. Effective teaching—United States. I. Title.
    LC4691.H457 2008
    371.9--dc22

                                                                    2008028499

10 9 8 7 6 5 4 3 2

Editorial and production services provided by
Hypertext Book and Journal Services
738 Saltillo St., San Antonio, TX 78207-6953 (210-227-6055)

Author's Dedication

This book is dedicated to my beautiful wife, Dardi. Your love for our children as well as the children who enter our lives hurting and lost is a model for which this book stands on. Thanks for doing the most important job there is: being a parent.

You are my best friend … You are everything to me.

Love, Joe

To the Reader

Why "wounded"? I have been involved with alternative education for most of my professional career ranging from teaching at juvenile lock-up facilities to being an alternative school principal. Through my many years of attending conferences and training sessions, the word "at-risk" has been used. I agree that there are many at-risk children in our society, but it became increasingly clearer to me that we are missing a real issue: Many of these children are not at-risk anymore. They are wounded. Their deep scars of emotional, physical, and mental pain are stuffed deep inside because, as a society, we are led to believe that they will go away.

As will be discussed in the book, I believe that some of the scars that our students are dealing with are internal, and they need to be brought to the surface because that is one of the ways to help reach wounded children. Once the scars are brought to the surface and dealt with, we can begin to reach these students at both emotional and cognitive levels.

This type of reaching out is uncomfortable for everyone because a lot of what comes to the surface is painful to hear, let alone deal with. However, it is essential for the healing process to start. Whatever your role in a child's education, understand that we all can be used as change agents to reach these students.

It is also important to realize that deep hurts affect every community, every state, and every nation regardless of race, gender, or economic status. It has no limits, not even age. Everyone has dealt with wounds in their life to some degree. It is how we respond to these wounds that takes us to a level of learning or despair. Like an emergency room physician, it is critical to deal with the wounds that cannot be ignored. This is not a time for prevention or evaluation but a time for action, and we must be well-trained and prepared. Someone once asked me what I am "selling" when I speak at seminars and my answer was simple: HOPE.

About the Author

Joe Hendershott, who resides in Ashland, Ohio, is a graduate of the Ohio State University in Columbus, Ohio, and holds a masters degree in school administration from Ashland University in Ashland, Ohio. His career spans more than 20 years as a teacher and school administrator.

Joe has an extensive background dealing with difficult and troubled youth in the school system. He has been a high school assistant principal, head principal, alternative school principal, and principal at Boys' Village School. Currently, Joe is the director of field experiences for the Schar College of Education at Ashland University where he also conducts professional development workshops designed to educate and empower those working with wounded children.

Joe and his wife, Dardi, are also cofounders of Hope 4 The Wounded, LLC (www.hope4thewounded.org), a consulting firm that targets working with wounded children and how to get them to academically achieve through various programs that include esteem building and emotional development. Joe has presented at national educational conferences as well as staff trainings. Joe speaks with passion about understanding the wounded students in our schools, and his diverse background gives him a unique perspective on this topic.

Our Vision: We believe that all children are valuable and can achieve their full potential when they are esteemed and empowered by grace, love and hope.

Our Mission: We desire to equip, empower and encourage those who are called to work with the broken and the lost children in this world.

Acknowledgments

I would like to thank some special people for their influence and encouragement during this journey. Without your inspiration, this book would not have been possible.

To my children Kaelee, Kearsten, Kameryn, Kyler, and Kade: Seeing your joy for life and that each of you have your own special gifts to give this world inspires me and blesses others. I am forever proud to call you my children. Thanks for giving our time for this book.

To "Punkie": You are a blessing.

To our foster children: Know that you have enriched my life and continue to stretch and teach me about the wounded children in our world. You will always have a forever family in our home.

To Gerald and Dorothy Lindecamp, Karl Angelo, and Terry Gerwig: Thank you for believing in this mission and supporting it from the beginning.

To my parents (Jack Hendershott and Jan Welsh) and family: Thank you for inspiring me to help others by your example.

To Dave and Deb Lash: It is an honor to be part of your family.

To Dan Fuller: What a privilege to start my career with a master teacher of wounded children. You taught me that it is not how big you are, it is how big your heart is that can make a difference.

To Bob Maruna: Thanks for giving a young college kid a break when he needed it most in his career and life. Your work with the hurting children in our society inspired me and defined the word "hope."

To Dr. Greg Gerrick: About all I can say is, "A teacher can make the difference in one person's life." It was an honor to have you as a teacher, but an even bigger honor to call you friend.

To Sandi Redenbach: Sometimes you meet someone in life who just makes a difference in all parts of your life. I am a better professional and person because of your teachings. I hope this book honors your work.

To the Wardle family (Terry, Cheryl, Aaron, and Destry): How much I value who you are and what you stand for. You have taught me so much with your insight and passion for those who are hurting and lost.

To Christa Lupo: Thank you for turning my chicken scratches into a manuscript.

Table of Contents

1

Understanding the Wounded Student

The Key to Reaching Wounded Students

"The marvelous richness of human experience would lose something of rewarding joy if there were no limitations to overcome. The hilltop hour would not be half so wonderful if there were no dark valleys to traverse."

~ Helen Keller

Several years ago, my wife, Dardi, was pulled over for speeding. Not only was she going over the speed limit, she was going over the speed limit in a school zone. Despite this, she managed to get off without a ticket. While I believe my wife is one of the most beautiful people in the world who can talk me into or out of just about anything, this is not what swayed the police officer. What he encountered was a frazzled woman with a 6-year-old child in the back seat who was bleeding profusely from his chin. My son was injured, and my wife was desperate to get him help.

The police officer had a choice to make. Dardi had clearly violated the rules of the road and faced punishment for this infraction. The officer could have ticketed her and would have been well within his rights. However, after assessing the situation, he determined that even though her actions were wrong (and he was quick to remind her of that), he understood her desperation to help her wounded child. My wife and son received a police escort to the hospital where my son received the treatment he needed. Due to a compassionate, caring officer who took the time to assess the situation and determine that it was unique, my son received help and was on the road to recovery.

In schools today, we are faced with critical situations that require quick thinking and the ability to assess a situation on an individual basis. As in the above scenario, the rules should be used as guidelines, not as absolutes. My child was not "at-risk" of being harmed; he was, indeed, a wounded child. Though in this case his wound was obviously a physical wound.

A lot of time is spent in public schools addressing at-risk students and how to best serve them. At-risk students definitely exist and can be defined as those who may not graduate on time or those who have trouble following the rules, a poor family life, a possible drug use/abuse problem, and so forth. The students I wish to address in this book are the students who are already wounded. These children are already bloodied by their past or present circumstances, and these circumstances have given them a sense of hopelessness. These children have been or are currently being abused or neglected, are depressed, live in poverty, or do not have parents or other adults who play a significant role in their lives.

How do we as a school system or individual work with the increasing number of students in this category? This is especially difficult in a new educational culture set up with state standards and "No Child Left Behind" where the attitude is that all students can and will achieve. This is a wonderful goal that is accurate in that all students *can* achieve. The second part of *will achieve* is the portion that concerns us as a system. The *will achieve* of this mission statement must be looked at closely for us to be successful when working with the wounded student. The purpose of this book is to make academic achievement the main focus of why we address the wounded student. If we do not keep the main thing the main thing (academic achievement), we will lose sight of our goals as educators. Many issues arise in our students lives that are sometimes beyond the students' or teachers' ability to change, and these issues have a direct impact on the learning process. Though it may be beyond our ability to change them, we can develop a new level of understanding that helps us deal with these issues and how it affects learning and achievement on an academic level.

How Can We Help?

First of all, what does a wounded student look like? How do we identify them to properly treat their educational needs? The wounded student is not subject to age, sex, race, or size/shape. However, one can easily be identified if we look to see if he or she has issues in the following areas: family/parents, personal/social skills, drugs, emotional problems, poor reasoning skills, lack of support, negative attitude about self and others, poor self-esteem, lack of past success in or out of school, et cetera. Our classrooms are full of students who resemble the above descriptions. How do we best serve all those needs in one classroom?

Even the most experienced and well-trained teacher can struggle with all these issues going on at once in a small setting such as the classroom.

The next step is to attempt to understand them. Remember that understanding is not excusing the act of wrongdoing. It merely explains why under certain circumstances students behave in a way that is not beneficial to themselves and others. Once we come to an understanding, we can start to respond to the students in a different way. The classic approach has not produced the results necessary to get these students ready to achieve. I have developed a new approach/attitude that I have found to be helpful to many: *I have to understand that I can't understand. There may be some level of understanding in some areas and possibly not in others.*

I was once brought a 15-year-old girl who had been found passed out from drugs in an alley near the school. I knew I might never understand why this young girl got to this point. I did not understand her past, family situation, peer group, and so on. However, what I did know was that she required immediate attention for her wounds, and that understanding may or may not come later. For this type of understanding, you should try not to judge the situation based on perception or from an angle of rules. We all know that certain rules have been broken and poor choices have been made. To pass judgment at this point only serves to compound the problem when what we desire is to head toward reaching and serving this student.

Teachers today are looking for new ways to help reach the children they serve. Teachers would be the first to admit that some of our kids are hurting and struggling in our schools. Teachers are also struggling with their students because they have chosen a profession that is designed to do what is right for the good of others. Teachers are service driven to help their students become better people as well as better students.

Through my years as a teacher and school administrator, I have seen many teachers reach out and help struggling students achieve amazing victories. I have seen teachers give unselfishly of their money with no expectation of reimbursement when a student was down and out. I have seen teachers drained of energy helping a student prepare for a test, a football game, band concert, or just helping a student get through his or her day. I have seen teachers volunteer countless resources to classrooms and students to make sure that the best learning environment is created. But most important, teachers give their time. Time is the most valuable gift a teacher can give to his or her students. Some of the greatest miracles of a child's life were made possible because a teacher gave the gift of time. With some of the answers being solved with time, this sets up the struggle that many educators have today. We know how important time is with students, but yet we are pulled in other areas that demand our time as well. Diminishing resources, testing, and documentation stretch us further away from time with our students.

Today's teachers are constantly looking for ways to provide this valuable time through their own training and/or professional development. Some teachers see it as a continuous personal quest to help their students achieve more than the students that came before them. Caring about all their students comes easy for teachers. This is what makes it a special profession: a fraternity of people dedicated to the good of others.

What We Can Do as Teachers

Throughout the book I hope it is clear that in no way can we be all things to all people as teachers or do I suggest we become psychologists, social workers, or police officers. It is extremely important to understand your limitations when working with young people. During the past couple years working with teachers across the country, I have witnessed great compassion from our teachers as they discuss, search, and even cry to find the answer to help children who are wounded. Trying to understand the students who enter the classroom wounded takes a new type of training and understanding. The students' wounds today seem bigger and deeper and in more abundance than in the past.

Teachers may not be the only answer for what a wounded student ultimately needs. However, a certain level of understanding and education on this topic can serve as a starting point for reaching many of these students and then guiding them in the right direction for professional assistance (social service or mental health agencies, etc.). Educators can provide encouragement and a basic level understanding of these wounds to direct our students to their path of success in and out of the classroom.

Teachers are successful professionals. They are driven by their ability to make others successful. I once heard it said at an educational conference that it is not just about being successful, it is about being significant. I believe this to be true for all educators. They are all significant in the lives of their students. Because of these qualities, teachers can be a new beginning for the wounded student.

Prevention

As educators, one of our goals should be to build strong children. This is not to suggest that all children are broken. But there are enough broken or wounded children in our schools to give us a call for conversation and a deeper look into the topic. One of my favorite quotes is from Frederick Douglass (2006): "It is easier to raise strong children than repair broken men." It is truly easier to work with issues earlier on in a child's life for prevention rather than repair them later. This is true of almost anything in our lives. This is why we do prevention measures with our homes, our cars, and even our physical health. Most of us understand this concept in our daily lives, but when it is looked at in educational terms we tend to fall short. We do not develop many programs for the truly at-risk or wounded students until high school age and then we try to repair the students with sometimes not very successful outcomes.

Educators must also understand that a wounded student's perspective on life is vastly different from their own. The way these students behave and live their young lives is often completely opposite to society's standards. Because of their past, their perspective is different as to what is acceptable. Again, the behavior does not have to be accepted by us, but it must be understood in order to reach this child to prepare them for academic success and future success in society. Their behaviors must change before they are adults in order for them to become a part of society.

When dealing with wounded students, it is also important to understand that these students bury their wounds as a survival tactic, so it becomes difficult to deal with such behaviors. Justice sometimes has already been applied to the life of a wounded child: we should simply treat the wound, not judge it.

School Policies

As a school system, we need to take a hard look at the most current research. It provides a clearer picture of the extent of what our schools are dealing with. For example, each day in America, we suspend 18,221 students from our public schools which results in more than 3 million students per school year (Children's Defense Fund, 2008a). Of course some of those 3 million suspensions are necessary when a child is a constant disruption to others or when weapons or drugs are the case. These issues are nonnegotiable and must be dealt with swiftly and seriously. However, my 20 years of experience as a teacher/ administrator in public and private schools has led me to ask, "Are all 3 million plus suspensions necessary?" I would guess that your experience has led you to the same answer I have come up with: No.

The problem is we deal with students in a way that was set up by board policies and procedures that try to be consistent and fair to all, which by its merit seems like the way to go. However, we are dealing with students who come into our schools who have been dealt different blows to their lives that are not consistent or fair.

How do we deal with these students when the policies are so black and white in our school handbooks? You must honor your school handbook/policies put into place by your local board of education, but you must also realize that these policies are put in place by teachers and administrators who take to the boards of education programs that are in the best interest of children within the schools. Based on the fact that more than 2,467 students a day are dropping out of our schools (Children's Defense Fund, 2008a), we may need to make some adjustments in our policies.

Giving Our Students Hope

Many of us we have come to the realization that we live in a nation of "stuffers." These are people who are taught at an early age to tough it out and stuff their hurts deep inside instead of talking about them. This works great on the surface for the wounded child because it is difficult to identify emotional wounds on the surface. However, wounds that are on the surface are much more easily identified—they may leave a scar, but scars are a sign of a healed wound.

Because most students have stuffed so many years of hurt inside, some wounds will be brought to the surface in many ugly ways (anger, depression, isolation, fear, anxiety, worry, or through many other issues). Notice some of the school violence that has taken place which has brought the need for antibullying character education. The truth is that unresolved anger turned inward could result in depression which is then expressed outward in aggression. Depression is reaching epidemic proportions in our nation.

One familiar example of a wounded person is Helen Keller. Helen was from a predominant family in the South in the late 1800s. At the age of 19 months, she was struck with an illness that left her blind and deaf. She grew into a child that was out of control. She had no real grasp of the world around her until her teacher, Miss Anne Mansfield Sullivan, came into her life when Helen was a few months short of turning 7 years old. Helen affectionately referred to Miss Mansfield Sullivan as "Teacher."

The rest of Helen Keller's life is the testimony to the power of a tolerant teacher who displayed amazing empathy, grace, mercy, and consistency wrapped around the relationship between teacher and student that is needed to work with wounded children. Helen went on to earn a BA degree and several honorary doctoral degrees from six universities throughout the world. She also wrote several books, including her story, "The Story of My Life," which was published in over 50 different languages. She went on to gain too many awards and honors to mention. When Helen died in 1961, Senator Listen Hill said during her eulogy that Helen showed the world there are no boundaries to courage and faith (American Foundation for the Blind, 2008).[1]

"The highest result of education is tolerance."
~Helen Keller

This saying accurately describes working with wounded children. The words are from someone of great courage and strength who overcame her own wounds to achieve great things. One of the reasons Helen was able to overcome those serious wounds was because of her teacher's ability to understand Helen's needs.

Many students are feeling lost and hopeless about the current state of affairs in their lives. As professional teachers, we try to instill hopes and dreams within our students. It is easy to assume that every child has expectations for their lives. However, in reality, it does not even occur to some of them to think about tomorrow. They struggle with just getting through today.

Turning a Mistake Into Success

This book could have been written about the number of mistakes I have made when trying to help a wounded student. I was doing what I thought at the time was in the best interest of the child only to find out later that it was not helpful at all to the student. My own failed attempts only served as a catalyst and a desire for more understanding of these children who desperately need their teachers to succeed. If I was going to be good to anyone, I had to be willing to search for answers in places I had not looked before. For this I went directly to the source: the wounded child. These changes led to the future success of other students, many resulting from what students had taught me.

---

1. American Foundation for the Blind Web site: www.afb.org

I believe as teachers we have our own successes and mistakes that we can all relate to and learn from. One of the issues that can be improved in education is to share our knowledge or experiences with other professional educators who you might be able to assist because of your efforts and successes working with students at any level. We need to take more time to celebrate the power we possess as teachers and the difference we can have on this world through education.

There is nothing as rewarding as seeing one of your students achieve at some level in or out of the classroom, and nothing can be as devastating as losing a student to poor grades, suspensions, dropping out, or not doing well in society. Many of the stories in this book are because I have been blessed to work with some teachers who have tried new ways of reaching hurting children in our schools. These stories are designed to lift up the true spirit of teaching.

The Rewards of Understanding

The following is an example of one of the first encounters I had as a principal dealing with a high school student. It was my first day as principal, and I was feeling pretty proud in my new position. Due to my lack of understanding of wounded children at the time, I was about to encounter a lesson I will never forget about the relationship between a wounded child and a teacher.

Bob came into the school wearing a hat (a handbook violation) and head phones (another violation). I approached Bob and said, "You cannot do those things in this school." After all, they were against the policies and procedures put in place by the board of education. I said for him to learn and achieve, he needed to remove those items immediately. Let's just say that the response by the student did not go well. He said, "Let me be clear. I don't like principals, I don't like school, I don't like you, and I will ignore you every day if you talk to me. I won't cause any problems and I will do my school work, but I want to be left alone." Wow! I thought, "I am the principal. He can't talk to me this way! Who does he think he his? I'm in control, not him."

After thinking about it for a bit, I remembered hearing once that nothing will destroy a relationship more quickly than ego and control. Before we jump to any conclusions, we need to think about that statement. Does anyone like to be controlled? Have you ever tried to control a spouse, friend, coworker, or family member? How would that go for your relationship? If we are honest, we will admit that control is the first step to destroying any relationship. Yet, sometimes as educators, we seem to think we must be in total control of the relationship for it to work. This is an upside down relationship philosophy.

So, I said to Bob, "I'll tell you what. I will allow you to be who you are, and I will be who I am. You can have your headset and hat in exchange for your behavior and school work. However, I have to be who I am, so I can't ignore you. Every day I will say hello to you." He said, "Fine. Everyday I will ignore you." And so it went. Every day I would say hello as I passed him in the hall, and every day he ignored me.

As time passed, Bob kept his word about behaving in school, causing no disruptions and doing his work. He would listen to the lessons from his teacher and then work silently by himself with his headset on. With the threat passing of either one of us having to be in control, we started to slowly develop trust which eventually led to conversation about his hopes and dreams (this was not an overnight process). Again, as with most wounded children, I found out it was hard for Bob to try to move forward because of his past experiences with his father, who at the time I met Bob, was in jail. The biggest influence in a child's life—good or bad—is the parent(s). The second biggest influence can be a teacher. For some wounded children, there is an absence of parental figures which moves the teacher into that number one slot of influence.

To finish this story with Bob, our relationship began in silence but evolved to one of trust over time. Because Bob had bounced around a lot, he never had an opportunity to have a job. The school assisted him in finding a position at a local restaurant where the manager was fine with the fact that Bob was not much into verbal communication. Eventually, Bob developed a good working relationship with the people around him and was made an assistant manager. Later, he was accepted into their management training program. Bob grew into his people skills, but more importantly he learned to trust. Bob has since left the restaurant business, reestablished his relationship with his father, and they are now in business together.

I tell this story for several reasons. First, it is important to understand that we cannot always understand where these students have been. By accepting this fact, we can keep ourselves from judging them. Bob was operating from a level of poor self-esteem and withdrawal as well as possible other issues. After some time, the reasons for this came to the surface.

Second, it is important that we operate from a position that every behavior is a teachable moment. We do not always have to apply punishment, but we can instead provide a meaningful learning experience. In Bob's case, it was the staff's ability to establish a relationship in a nonjudgmental way that opened the door to positive opportunities for this young man.

Throughout this process, it was critical to ask questions about how I could help versus, "Why do you behave that way?" We must constantly remind ourselves that we are not the focus of our chosen profession (I choose to refer to teaching as a calling). Teaching is about service to others.

The Power of One Teacher

Wounded children are hurt and do not understand how the wounds that none of us can see are affecting their development. Wounds are hidden deep in the subconscious mind resulting in many different types of dysfunctional behaviors. If collectively we, as educators, begin to identify these deep hurts in our youth, then we can get to the teaching part. Reaching the student will lead to hope, and where there is a sense of hope, the sky is the limit for academic and life success.

Learning cannot make sense to these children until we have restored hope in their broken lives. Remember, it only takes one teacher to turn a child's life around. The power we have as teachers is incredible, but unfortunately it is not a profession that is always valued as it should be in our culture. Sometimes we buy into the statement "I am ONLY a teacher, so there is not much I can do." My desire is to transform the educational system by simply turning this statement around to the truth: "There is a lot I can do because I am a teacher. I will not surrender my power to anyone during a teachable moment, and every behavior gives an opportunity to teach."

Think for a moment about what a major effect this statement would have on our students. How can we expect to empower wounded children to turn their lives around if we don't empower ourselves and our profession? Teaching is an honorable profession filled with caring people who are working against incredible odds. In the professional sports arena, we call these people heroes. Maybe it is time for a new definition of hero in our culture.

The Bottom Line

The first time I spoke on this topic was to be with an audience of 25-50 people at a conference in Florida. By the time I arrived, the session had grown to almost a thousand people and had to take place in the grand ballroom of the conference center. They were there because they were desperate for information on this topic. Everyone has seen it, but we have few strategies on how to deal with it. It becomes increasingly clear that this is about the cry for help from our educators and society. I have had calls to speak at preschools, elementary conferences, middle school and secondary conferences, universities, and maximum security prisons. The need is everywhere. I encourage you to continue to have conversations on this topic because you will be the answer to your school's needs and programs for the wounded students in your district.

It also makes sense to look at this as a benefit to overall society. Reforming public education and keeping students in school instead of suspending them increases student achievement and graduation rates as well as decreases dropout rates. A 5% increase in graduation rate and college matriculation of just the male student population could lead to a combined savings and revenue of almost $8 billion a year for our nation's economy. In addition, the nation's crime-related costs would be significantly reduced (Alliance for Excellence in Education, 2006). Our schools should be viewed as community centers of caring and achievement for all children. For our students to become productive, caring citizens, it is imperative to understand that "modeling is the greatest form of teaching."

Chapter 1 Key Points

- ♦ It is best to understand that we can't understand where many of these students are coming from.
- ♦ Do not judge wounded children.
- ♦ Deliver meaningful discipline, not punishment.
- ♦ Know the biggest factor for student success is the parent(s), good or bad.
- ♦ Wounded children have low self-esteem and poor reasoning skills.
- ♦ Don't ask "Why?"; instead, ask what you can do to help.
- ♦ Wounds need to be brought to the surface. Sometimes this takes time, patience and developing a trusting relationship.
- ♦ Let go of ego and control which destroys relationships.
- ♦ Restore hope.
- ♦ Hendershott model for reaching wounded students:

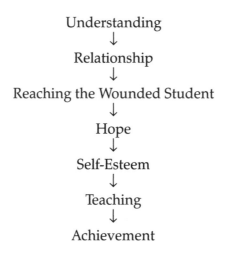

Understanding
↓
Relationship
↓
Reaching the Wounded Student
↓
Hope
↓
Self-Esteem
↓
Teaching
↓
Achievement

2

Identifying the Wounded Student

The Diversity of Wounded Students

"There's nothing so rewarding as to make people realize they are worthwhile in this world"
> ~ Bob Anderson, English Poet

I have had the privilege of working with some excellent elementary school teachers over the years, and I have had the advantage of being an elementary school teacher and certified administrator. Through my relations and experiences, I believe that one resource we sometimes neglect in our system is the voice of these early childhood teachers. These teachers are the first to pick up on a student's needs. If we are going to change the old way of doing business, we must empower the input of those on the front line, thus identifying these wounded students at an early age.

As an alternative secondary education principal, I constantly heard from elementary teachers who told me that they could predict who I would be seeing at the alternative school in a few years. Later, when I started to work with these teachers, they began to tell me what a wounded student looks like at an early age and how they came to that conclusion:

- ◆ **Family/Parent Structure:** This is the number one indicator that potentially spells out academic failure for students.

- ◆ **Personal Social Skills:** Already students had struggles in this area based on what they had experienced and learned outside of school.

- ◆ **Drugs, including a family history of drug abuse or use**: Elementary teachers really get to know their children on a more intimate level than perhaps a high school teacher, who may only see the student 45 minutes to an hour each day.

- ◆ **Emotional Problems:** The inability to put basic emotional skills to use in handling constructive teaching or peer relations and often withdrawing from their peers.

- ◆ **Poor Reasoning Skills**: Making poor choices at an early age leads to bigger issues or consequences for poor reasoning/choice-making in the future. This lack of guidance needs to be changed so that the teachers and role models are working to get their students to the critical thinking stage.

- ♦ **Lack of Support**: Family and poor social structure is already visible at a young age. Waiting will only make the problem more difficult to handle.

The Many Faces of the Wounded Student

We often think of the wounded student as a child in a lower social economic, single-parent home. Though this description may fit some, it only begins to explain what a wounded student may look like. The wounded student does not have a particular age, gender, race, or nationality. He or she can be from all walks of life. The constant among all wounded children, meaning the factor that defines how we view them, is the failure to achieve academic success and what gets in the wounded child's way of academic success. Why can our elementary teachers easily identify these students at such an early age, but we fail to reach them or change their path to academic failure?

The wounds of these students can range from mild to severe. Regardless of the wound, it must be treated with the proper prescription. Some students will require a longer process to reach those wounds with intensive sustained care, while others, if identified at an early age, can be reached in a faster fashion. Early intervention is the key.

The problem with the identification of these students and their wounds is that they are scarred from the inside. An injury on the surface can be identified quickly and accurately so healing can begin; internal scars are not visible, thus harder to determine and treat. The unknown cannot be treated. The problem is not that our teachers do not care and are not trying, the problem is that the tools we have been given or trained in are not absolutes to student success. When a student is tested, we set a level of expectation based on those results. Again, this test can set a child up for an area of academic wounding. If the test says it, it must be so.

Much has been made in our schools about the need for rules, handbooks, and guidelines for students. Again, we want to give students something that can pinpoint their failure: a guideline that would be impossible for many students to follow to the letter. We tell them to sit down, be quiet, and pay attention; all other behaviors are not accepted. These rules are very cold and are only a calculated way of educating/creating a culture of distrust and barriers: we talk about diversity and then try to treat everyone the same. Handbooks are well meaning, but can be so rigid that it can spell disaster for many students. I want to be sure that the following point is made regarding handbooks and rules: I believe that the current rules in place by the board of education in every district needs to be followed by everyone who works in the school district. However, I am trying to make the point that as teachers, if you feel a policy is not helping students, beneficial, or is outdated due to new research and information, you can work with your administration and school board to facilitate a possible change.

A wounded student may look like fear or anxiety, or she or he may carry the look of stress from depression and anger. These internal triggers cross all sex, racial, and social economic boundaries. Triggers can portray themselves in the forms of low self-esteem, poor social skills, emotional problems, and drug abuse to hide the pain.

The teaching profession needs more and better ways to properly identify our students. We continuously use the term *at-risk* while the truth is, these are wounded children who disguise themselves rather well. The programs for at-risk students are effective for those students who are truly at-risk and not wounded. Some students just need some extra help in school or areas of their lives that, if left untreated, could result in a further downfall in performance academically. The behaviors exhibited by an at-risk student and a wounded child can sometimes be hard to distinguish. I believe the biggest difference is that a wounded child has deeper emotional scars than those students who are at risk. Most people have some level of emotional scars. It is just that a wounded child's scars are more severe or have never been dealt with properly allowing these wounds to cause further damage.

One suggestion I have to anyone trying to identify a wounded student is to ask them, "What are your hopes and dreams?" A wounded child will just look at you with a strange look or blank stare. This question is totally foreign to their thought process. Not only are wounded children trying to figure out how to get through today, they are also trying to figure out how to deal with their past. The future to some might only seem like a bleak possibility. If a student has no hopes and dreams, how can an education make sense to them? What would be the point? We all know that for students to achieve, an education must make sense in their lives. Memorization of textbooks or materials has no practical application to the wounded child's life.

The Importance of Relationships in the Wounded Student's Life

Some of the at-risk programs do effectively deal with some of those emotional issues before they become bigger issues for those students. Prevention and the use of your professional counselors to help in these areas are crucial. During my first year of teaching in Florida, I had a student who, by all outward appearances, had everything going for him. He came from a family that could afford to send him to one of the nicest private schools in the South. After getting to know this student, I found out that he was dealing with issues that I could not help him overcome at that point in his life. I believed in him as a teacher and coach and saw the incredible potential he had as a young man. Additionally, this student was also very intelligent, talented, and personable, but at that point in his life he was not living up to those skills. This young man probably could have walked into any college campus as an athlete and been given a full scholarship. The negative power of his wounds combined with my lack of understanding for how to identify, help, or reach him left us both defenseless.

Twenty years after working with that young man as his teacher and coach, and after not talking to him for probably 15 years, I received a phone call from him. He explained to me that he has never married and is currently serving in the military and may have to return to the war soon. The details to which he described his life and call to duty proved of the man he has become; he is a credit and true hero to this country. Our phone call was very emotional on both ends and left us making plans to reunite.

For this young man to want to continue a relationship some 15 to 20 years later truly shows the power a teacher can have on his or her students. He has become a man who has turned his life into a role model for his country. I hope our new relationship will allow us to become even greater friends and support for one another. He was excited to hear my passion for helping teachers become better prepared for helping students identify their wounds and to provide earlier intervention than he had received.

It is well known that our elementary school teachers are very relationship driven. One of the reasons for this is simply that they have to be based on the high needs of children at this age. Like a child in your home, you spend a majority of your time with your students when they are young out of necessity for their safety and growth, while meeting most, if not all, of their emotional needs. As children or students mature into adulthood, our constant nurturing is not as necessary if we have invested properly in their growth at a very young age.

Wounded children can be identified at an early age, where we have wonderful, talented, and caring teachers who possess the proper training and resources to begin delivering the care needed to reach the child. In this way, we are not waiting 6 more years until they get to our alternative high schools, when the damage has already been inflicted to a level of major proportions.

Later in the book you will see specific programs that have worked in elementary schools that were developed for the early detection of wounds and the addressing of those wounds with professionally trained people. These programs also involve the parents and teachers and set up a culture beyond the school day that says we care about the success of your child in our school and that your child is valued and we will give you and your child hope for a bright future.

The Inward Signs of a Wounded Student

One thing that I continue to discover is that there is no one key factor to look for when asking the question: What does a wounded child look like? The wounded child can be your star football player on Friday night, your young lady singing in the school choir, or anyone who is trying to hide the pain that is hidden deep inside. Students do not have to be in a juvenile lock up facility or have a criminal record to be wounded. Some students who have been wounded develop a wide range of unhealthy coping strategies to help hide their pain and prevent the pain from returning.

Withdraw: Children have a natural response to withdraw from what is causing them pain. The pain can cause them to be runaways trying to get away from a home life that it harmful. It can be the use of drugs in an attempt to cover up pain. It can also be students who are skipping school because they are not able to concentrate on academics because the adult influences in their lives have not set a value of education in their life.

Stress: Students who have layers of stress around them are sometimes very wounded children. Sometimes students tend to take on not only their own stress but their parents' or family's stress as well. The problem with children and stress is that they do not have the coping skills like adults do to deal with stress. And some wounded children are around adults who do not have those coping skills for stress, so students try to wear both their parents' stress as well as their own.

Anger: We start to see anger and then it can manifest itself in so many different ways. We see plenty of angry kids in our hallways and classrooms. We see anger in the way students talk to their teachers and classmates. These behaviors can be violent such as kicking, striking, or assaulting others (when students are at this level, it is good to have de-escalation training for your staff to keep situations like this under control before things get out of hand and someone gets hurt). When we become upset and deal with anger with our own frustrations, it can become a very bad situation.

Bonding or Relationship Issues: Many students who have been wounded have a difficult time developing trusting relationships with almost anyone. They have been hurt so badly in the past that they only expect the same in the future. Because of the time we have with our students on a daily basis, especially in the younger years, we can have a profound effect in this area. Just giving students familiar routines where they feel safe can help and some trust can start to be restored. Many of these students feel detached from their families so it is hard for them to attach to new people This lack of trust can start at a very early age and can linger a lifetime.

Obsessive Compulsive: These students feel that if they can completely control a situation, then maybe nothing bad will happen. They are very attentive to details and do everything they can to control you and their surroundings.

Depression: This is one area that we should definitely not take on. I believe it is vital that we are trained to look for warning signs of depression in our children, but if we suspect a child is dealing with any level of depression, they need to be referred to a person who is a licensed, trained professional in this area. Depression itself is a whole subject that has many different faces, and the numbers are increasing in all levels of our society from adults to your children.

More students today are seeking assistance for depression which can also be a reason for the increase. What is difficult to determine is how many students are out there who do not have resources to get the help they may need. Below are some warning signs of depression:

- low self-esteem;
- students who are isolated;
- anger or increase in anger;
- students who feel hopeless;
- students who act sad or look sad;
- anxiety;
- fear;
- apathy;
- concentration could be low;
- school attendance drops/lack of interest;

- ◆ students who injure themselves; and/or
- ◆ drug or alcohol abuse/students who try to self medicate.

The above signs may be indications that something is seriously wrong and needs to be addressed by a trained professional in the area of depression. There may be other signs as well. There are some schools that are training a counselor or hiring a counselor from the outside to help with screening and then getting the parents and trained licensed professionals to assist the students.

The fact that you care enough to help identify a student who may be hurting in your class and then getting them the professional help they need is key to the recovery process. In the absence of parents, teachers may be the only ones who can identify and get help for these students. Teachers spend more time with these young people than anyone else in their lives. A lot of these students look like your straight-A student. In other words, your straight-A student can be wounded as well.

A good way to look at the teaching profession is to not just call ourselves teachers. There are many other names that fit:

- ◆ friend;
- ◆ guide;
- ◆ social servant;
- ◆ navigator;
- ◆ pioneer;
- ◆ artist;
- ◆ composer;
- ◆ advocate;
- ◆ role model;
- ◆ leader;
- ◆ cheerleader; and
- ◆ visionary.

The list can go on and on. An educator inspires young people to achieve their hopes and dreams, and we all know that it takes more than one approach to deliver this message of hope into the lives of young people.

The Bottom Line

In closing, this was probably the most important chapter because it establishes the difficulty of working with wounded children. There are no definite physical signs that lead one to believe that another person is wounded. As discussed, there are several other indicators that address what a wounded student can look like. These are more behavioral and emotional indicators, such as depression, anger, withdrawal, and so on. As a system, we need to set up training that will provide our educators with the means to report these indicators and start to deal with them as early as preschool and all the way up to our adult education programs.

During my 6 years working as an educator in a juvenile lock up facility, I spoke to several hundred students throughout the years. The one common trait was that, although some looked like they were okay, conversations revealed deep scars that led them to detention. The number one thing each child would say to me was that if he had just had someone who cared, then he may not be there. At first, I honestly believed that this was just an excuse that these students were using to avoid taking responsibility for their actions or behaviors. But as the conversations developed, I found it to be true more often than not.

Chapter Two Key Points

- ◆ The outward appearance of a wounded student has no definite characteristics.
- ◆ Involve your elementary schools in early identification and training working with wounded children.
- ◆ Identify the wound specifically—emotional, physical, family, social, et cetera. Identifying is different than labeling.

- ◆ Internal wounds are identified by behaviors, not physically.
- ◆ Go beyond the regular evaluation process, that is, standards, tests, and so on.
- ◆ Develop rules that are designed to say your achievement is important to us.
- ◆ Develop programs that speak to hope for the children and families.
- ◆ Get professional help when working with serious emotional issues such as depression.

3

The Current State of Schools

The One-Third Model

"You cannot do a kindness too soon because you never know how soon will be too late."
~ Ralph Waldo Emerson, American Writer/Poet

Based on the current research on student achievement and high suspension and drop out rates, it is easy to see that our schools are in need of a fundamental redesign to meet the needs of all students. We are all making progress and doing a greater amount of research and data collecting to help lead these reforms. What also needs to be taken into account is information regarding our children that cannot be collected or calculated such as a student's emotional needs and esteem issues. Until we consider this along with the numbers and standards and research, we will continue to stray into what I call a one-third model of education.

The One-Third Model

The schools are and have been traditionally designed for what I call the top one-third students, or the academic minded. There is nothing wrong with the top one-third students being success-ful. They are fun to teach, easy to be around, and they can also challenge us intellectually. Most of these students will do what needs to be done to get to the next level of achievement. But these students only reflect the academic portion of school suc-cess. Even the top third of students may have emotional wounds. These students might achieve more if this understand-ing of emotional wounds applied to all students.

The middle one third is what I call the survivors—they can go up or down in this model. They are the quiet type. They are going to make it because they know how to adapt to their sur-roundings to get by. Many of these students could be categorized as possible "at-risk" students. They could get lost in the system, be potential dropouts, or have attendance issues. The middle third of students have wounds to deal with as well. If we understand that these students are at the tipping point of success or failure, then our ability to have a deeper understanding of the emotional state of these at-risk students could determine their academic success or failure.

I spoke with the district representative of one school about this issue of helping the at risk/survivor type of student and was told that they had no time to address this type of program because it does not immediately address the academic needs of these students. I was told that it was their priority to get scores up right away, and that it wasn't the right time. I can appreciate the pressure on schools today to score well on achievement tests, but you cannot have real change in student achievement and in the student's overall well-being without addressing the whole child.

The bottom one third is what I call our wounded children. These are students who might not make it without our understanding. They are students in need of our critical care. They need the ability to see the current value of education in their overall life. The bottom third of students have a difficult time academically because our educational structure does not normally take into account the issues they are facing. The idea that wounded students can reach their academic potential without schools addressing or at least having an understanding of the student's issues needs to be rethought. This is an area where our trained school counselors could be of great assistance because they should have the basic understanding of how the issues these students are facing is intertwined with their ability to achieve academic success.

Our data collection and standards do not reflect these needs. If a student is struggling with problems in their life, they are still required to take tests on certain days. This style of testing on paper seems like a level playing field for all students, but what about students who we know are not ready to test? I believe the system does care, but we need to move into a model that reflects the good for the overall student body. It is important to measure where a student is academically and what areas need to be improved, but testing will not provide an accurate picture of the student's ability if the student is struggling with deep emotional wounds.

The Changing Model

Although I believe this one-third model to be a true picture of the current state of school structure, I have noticed the model begin to change over the past few years. In the next 5 years I believe it will more closely resemble a one-third and two-thirds model. I believe that the gap between the top third and lower one third is becoming increasingly wider and the middle one third is slowly moving toward the bottom one third. There are likely several reasons for this change, but I believe the biggest reason is the increasing poverty level in our country. There is becoming a greater gap between the haves and all the have-nots.

In 2006, nearly 37 million people (12.3%) were in poverty, 12.8 million (17.4%) children under the age of 18 were in poverty and 7.6 million (9.8%) families were in poverty (America's Second Harvest, The Nation's Food Bank Network, 2006).

The Top Third and the Bottom Third

Let's take a look at some of the differences between the top one third and the bottom one third. What are some areas that need to be taught along with the current content areas to help wounded students? Wounded students need to be taught some of the following skills:

- ♦ listening skills;
- ♦ communication skills;
- ♦ organization skills;
- ♦ detail skills;
- ♦ time management skills;
- ♦ emotional skills;
- ♦ critical thinking skills; and/or
- ♦ goal setting skills.

Many of your top one-third students are able to concentrate on their academics because some of the above have already been mastered. However, any student at any level can carry wounds. Even students in the top one third can carry wounds that can get in the way of them achieving more than they already have. Wounds that are not dealt with will flair up at some point in the child's life. It is easier to identify them and deal with them before you are in a state of emergency. Sometimes not dealing with their wounds can cost them their colleges, friends, family, or possibly jobs.

Let's take a good look at what a classroom for the top one third might look like. Anyone could walk by and if the classroom is quiet and under control, we believe that learning is taking place. With good classroom management you can find those elements at times, but it is sometimes measured as the second biggest important factor. I have seen plenty of very quiet rooms with minimal disruption where little, if any, learning is actually taking place. If wounded children or any child is to work on their social skills, listening skills, and communication skills, how can they do this in a plastic bubble or plastic environment?

Likewise, if you walk by a room and hear some noise and students are out of their seats, there is a natural assumption that the teacher does not have control of his or her class. When, in fact, this type of interaction can be the type of environment the bottom two third of the students may need to keep them engaged in the class and school overall. This type of interaction can happen regularly when working with students in career lab settings. The students would be involved in their career labs for close to 3 hours and because they were engaged, up out of their seats, and the learning had a practical application to their lives, they had very few behavior problems. Again, no situation is 100% perfect either way. But those same students who just spent close to 3 hours in one classroom lab would go to their academic part of the day and you would start to find a completely different type of behavior from them. Understanding learning styles is critical to teaching on any level.

The Role of Learning Styles

We can, in some classrooms, forget the students' learning styles and what adjustments needed to be made for their learning. Those teachers who understood students' learning styles

and made those adjustments had higher achievement, attendance, and created a positive learning environment. Many times
while working in a juvenile detention center I was reminded
how critical it is to consider individual learning styles and still
develop a class structure that reinforces academic achievement.
I found that all students enjoyed academic achievement once
they were focused and I had a basic understanding of who they
were and what their potential was as students.

I use the example all the time that teaching is all about being
a good coach. When you look at your successful coaches, they
are able to take each team, year in and year out, and make a
game plan based on each team's individuals' strengths and
weaknesses. If as a coach you only coach one way and do not
make adjustments, you will be doomed to failure. In fact, during
every game you hear the announcers say, "What adjustments
will the coach make at halftime?" Not only is it talked about, it is
expected. Each coach understands his or her players and will
treat them all differently within the team structure so they can
be successful.

A coach may yell in one player's face because he knows that
the player is motivated by this type of interaction, but to the next
player the coach may respond calmly by setting him on the
bench and talking to him for a few minutes because the coach
knows that same "yelling" approach used on this player would
only cause him to crumble. Many wounded students in the bottom two thirds emotionally are like this second type of athlete.
Yelling and screaming does not work for them. This has been
tried and it just sinks them deeper emotionally and does not
help rebuild their esteem.

We expect this type of adjustment on our athletic fields, but
not in our classrooms. I have seen several teachers who can make
these adjustments and therefore become more successful with
their students. They set up a win-win situation for every student.

Allowing for Flexibility

It is critical to understand that just because you make adjustments does not mean that you do not have clear expectations.
Make your goals for each classroom and student clear and

achievable. We develop handbooks that say everyone will come in and learn this way, and if the handbook does not look a certain way, it cannot be successful. Almost every school that I have come into contact with has very lengthy and hard to understand handbooks. Many wounded students will look at these handbooks at the beginning of the year and realize from the start that they have very little chance of being successful.

Handbooks should be clear and easy to read. Boundaries for all students need to be made clear for the safety of students as well as for others, but they can be stated so that students know that we will work with them. We can hold our students accountable and still treat them with dignity. When you use phrases like "will be suspended," it can really tie our hands. Instead, say that a suspension may or could result because each situation has its unique story. This change will allow some flexibility. It is good to help all students build a sense of responsibility and desire to follow guidelines. This can help with esteem as long as it is done with the right kind of approach, such as meaningful consequences, instead of just discipline that lacks meaning.

As teachers, it is extremely important to make sure we have a full picture of who our customers are: the students. There is no business in the world that is successful that does not pay full attention to their customers and who they are. We must look at:

- ◆ What makes them think?
- ◆ What makes them feel?
- ◆ What motivates them?
- ◆ How can we better serve them?
- ◆ How can we improve our customer service?

One of the most important jobs any businessman has is figuring out how to keep their customers. This should also be the goal of our schools where, instead, the current structure continues to set up barriers that are causing us to quickly lose our customers. Every second a student in public schools is suspended and every 10 seconds a high school student drops out (Children's Defense Fund, 2008b).

We have to stop taking for granted that policy and procedure books will be all these students need to get through school. These policies and procedures are important and we must keep them, but they need to be updated to truly reflect our students and their needs. Anyone who works in our schools today has a realistic picture of who our students are and realizes how difficult it can be to make the current handbooks reflect the needs for every student academically and behaviorally. We should develop policies that reflect what our students are facing when they enter our classrooms. Every community and school is different and you can be the person to help formulate a model that will work for the betterment of student success for all students based on the students' needs.

Sometimes we look for outside programs or universal models that we can implement. Outside models can be used, but they must fit your school culture and no one knows the students in your building better than you do. You are the expert needed for the fundamental redesign to change within your school.

Understanding Behavior Triggers

Remember, every behavior is a teachable moment. We need to look at these moments as opportunities for students to learn control and listening and communication skills in an appropriate manner. Having an expert in the area of children who are wounded can assist you to set up clear guidelines of expectations for all students. This person can keep your policies from being unknowing triggers for even bigger behaviors. For example, if you have a policy that says that each student should be given some space when being dealt with, this can help with students who have been abused. Space issues can cause triggers in the students, thus causing them to be more angry or defensive when dealing with a simple behavior. People who have space issues are triggers for everyone, and we as adults do not like people invading our personal space. Therefore, a student who has those triggers can be especially sensitive to space issues.

Sometimes for the safety of the student or others, the space has to be invaded. Setting policies that say we want to approach you in a safe and understanding manner help to keep the situation from escalating. Training for the entire staff in this area of de-escalation can be a wonderful tool for the staff. De-escalation skills are essential skills in alternative school settings and when working with students who are emotionally wounded.

Some situations turn into much more than they should because a staff member unknowingly sets off some trigger in the student. Training is vital to keeping your own staff safe as well. We certainly do not want to put anyone in a position in which they feel trapped causing them to act in a defensive manner.

What are some of the emotions that we can identify in wounded students that we need to be aware of and have training in as educators? Not that we need to be experts in these areas, in fact we cannot be, but we should have at least a general working knowledge in some of the following areas:

♦ aggressive students;

♦ students who abuse themselves;

♦ suicide;

♦ bullying;

♦ withdrawn students;

♦ students who have been abused;

♦ students who have been neglected; and/or

♦ emotional/esteem issues.

A general working knowledge in these areas will give you a much clearer picture of who your students are and what it will take for us to have a better understanding of what they are dealing with.

Some of your staff, such as school counselors or your intervention staff, may have some training in these areas. Use their area of expertise to train the staff. Do not just send all of the kids to them. The numbers alone can be overwhelming for anyone to deal with alone. Again, sending them to school administrators does not guarantee that they will have any more training or understanding with wounded children than you do yourself. That is why it is so important to train the whole staff to have a general working knowledge of how to deal with emotionally wounded children.

Other Approaches to Consider

There are many things to keep in mind when building a new model within your school. First of all, kids who develop good and positive relationships with your school teachers tend to communicate better about their own lives as well as what they know within the school. When they develop a certain level of trust, they will talk about others who may need assistance, or have information to help keep the school safe. If they feel that they can be heard, they will help with keeping the environment safe for you and others. If kids feel like they can't trust you with this information, then they will not talk.

Second, prevention is the key to helping these students. We know that they have had some kind of trauma in their young lives, so our responsibility is to set up programs that will prevent further damage to their wounds. We tend to concentrate on things like how many video cameras we can purchase to view as many of the halls as possible, and can we afford metal detectors or have at least one police officer to protect all of us if needed.

These are the issues or tools that we resort to or that come to mind when we talk about prevention. These are indeed a help but they do set a tone of: "We don't know how to handle you anymore, so we will catch you on film so that you can't deny anything." Or, "We will hire someone who has the force to control you." Or, "Because we distrust a few, we will not trust anyone."

It is a much better approach to establish prevention programs that say we will be in the halls with you so the need for cameras is not as important as our involvement. Our interaction could be sufficient. It should be understood that some schools have had major cuts in faculty and staff and sometimes the cameras will be a useful tool to keep everyone safe. Develop programs that say we know who is not following the rules, and we will deal with them and not set up distrust issues for everyone.

Set up programs for student improvement in all areas: academic, emotional, and behavioral. Set up programs that deal with the specific areas of improvement that your school needs. We need to do away with the old system of detention and suspension that punishes and does not teach. Just because we have always done things a certain way, does not mean that we have to continue them if they are ineffective in helping children achieve the lifelong skills they need.

Other important areas to research within your school are in the areas of music, art, or play therapy. These areas are of significant benefit as ways for students to communicate how they are feeling or thinking about the past, present, or future.

The wonderful possibilities to help wounded students are endless because everyone is made up of a variety of years of experience and different backgrounds. We can come up with solutions that are new and exciting as well as having the experience of putting new ideas into practice. Students are counting on our ability to gain new knowledge in the area of behavioral, emotional, and academic skills. Even though it looks like wounded children only happen at the bottom one third, you may also have children suffering in the top one third. Children who have been wounded by neglect, abuse, or trauma of some kind in their young lives can come from any group. The advantage to these programs is that they will help the top one third as well as the middle and the bottom one third.

The Bottom Line

The hope is that this chapter provided you with some personal and professional hope. You are the expert for your children. They need you and are counting on you. If you see something that is not working for students and is causing you great frustration, then you are looking at a program that does not work. Take the new information you have been given and start new programs to benefit all students.

I would be pleased that within a few years this chapter has to be removed from this book or revised because schools meet the needs of all students in all areas, not just thirds. All students should be placed under one category, and that category is those who are meeting their full potential on an emotional and academic level.

Chapter 3 Key Points

- ◆ Schools are divided in thirds and best serve the top academic one third of students.
- ◆ The middle third of students in our schools are survivors. They are at-risk type of students.
- ◆ The bottom third of students struggle emotionally, behaviorally, and academically.
- ◆ Staff need to be trained in de-escalation skills.
- ◆ Develop prevention programs in elementary schools.

4

Why Address the Wounded Student

What Is Your Mission and Vision for Wounded Students?

"You cannot live the perfect day without doing something for someone who will never be able to repay you."
~ Sam Rutigliano, NFL Coach

Take a moment before you continue in this chapter and think of all the reasons to address wounded students. Your reason for addressing these students may be different than someone else, but the end result should be student achievement. I hear from many students and teachers about their wounds that happened in the schools. The list is too long to put down. I am sure as we look back on our school years from kindergarten through college, we have very strong opinions about our teachers one way or the other. When I ask teachers to describe their experience with other teachers, I hear many wonderful things: they were really nice, they really cared, they made a difference in my life, I want to be just like my teacher. Notice how they do not say first off that they taught me math or that they really knew their English, what they talk about is the emotional connection. These emotionally healthy environments created a safe nurturing environment to learn math, English, or health. Without addressing the emotional part, it is tough to get to the academic achievement portion. Again, I do hear those connectors to the cognitive learning piece, but it always seems to come after they describe how their teacher made them feel.

Academic Achievement

The first reason to address the wounded student is academic achievement. If we do not take the time necessary to address the wounded student's emotions, they will not achieve academically to their potential. Wounded children are bound up with stress, anxiety, anger, and fear. All of these emotions get in the way of learning.

In an article on children and stress (Hill, 2008), Hill states that children can be even more affected by stress than adults can. What's more is they put up with our stress and develop their own from it. Stress interferes with short-term memory, which is electrical in form and very easily disrupted. It is housed in the limbic system, where all information flows in and out of the brain. Stress interrupts this flow of information therefore disrupts learning and memory. This is one reason why we must create a positive learning environment free of stress and fear of failure. We must create an environment that says it is okay to make mistakes. We are in school to learn, not to be perfect.

Increase Student Attendance

The second reason why we should address wounded students is to increase attendance. Many alternative schools have been able to increase attendance because the teachers have received the proper training to understand the students' needs and then address them in a positive learning environment. Students start to attend because they become connected with their teachers and so students are more open to what they are being taught. Many programs I have seen increase from an attendance rate of around 70% to around 93 to 95%. Without attendance, the students are not there to learn. How many of us would want to attend our place of work if we did not feel respected, wanted, or invited?

Many enjoy going home at night because we like to be in a place that is welcoming to us and full of people who are happy to see us when we walk through the door. If we want to increase achievement, we must create an environment that welcomes students and tells them we are happy to see them. Many of us have this when entering school, but there are some students we do not understand, so it is easier to not have them in attendance instead of taking on the challenge of creating an environment that welcomes everyone—problems and all. If kids do not find acceptance at home or school, they will find a place that does accept them. When attendance drops, the risk of dropping out increases.

Decrease Student Dropout Rates

The third reason to address the wounded student is to decrease the dropout rate. There are many reasons why students drop out of school:

1. The student does not feel connected.
2. The student has low self-esteem.
3. The student has a high suspension/expulsion rate.
4. The student does not feel physically (bullying) or emotionally safe or secure.
5. The material is not relevant to the student's life.
6. Family issues.
7. Financial reasons.
8. Substance abuse.

It is also important that we pay attention to the dropout rate of students with disabilities. "Dropout is most prevalent among youths with learning disabilities and serious emotional disturbances" (Bost, 2008).

I make this reference to ensure that we all understand the importance of understanding students who are wounded emotionally. A deeper understanding and training for all teachers in this area and in our teacher college preprograms can have a profound impact on reducing this rate. I believe that the reason students with disabilities have a higher dropout rate is not because we do not care; it is an issue of understanding.

According to Alliance for Excellence in Education (n.d.-a), only about 70% of all high school students graduate on time. If we take a look at these numbers, it is easy to conclude that something is wrong with our current policies and precedence regarding our students who have disabilities or behavior problems. We must develop programs that deal with keeping our students in school, in the classroom, and say to our students that we miss you when you are not at school. These numbers affect all of us. An increase in graduation rate would add billions to our national economy as well as cut crime in our communities.

Decrease Suspensions and Expulsions

The fourth reason we need to address the wounded student is to decrease suspensions and expulsions. Much of this goes along with the previous research stated. We know that when students are removed from our buildings, it increases their chance of dropping out. We have to understand that students do not just wake up one morning and decide to drop out. They have had repeated behavior issues, a history of poor grades, and attendance and suspension issues. These problems have reached the point where the student just gives up, and they are not helped properly due to the lack of programs and support.

Unless students are bringing guns, weapons, drugs, or violence, we need to figure out ways to deal with the behavior to keep them in our schools. There are instances when the time a student spends away from school during a suspension can help the school and student to figure out a plan of success. So suspensions in some cases are necessary. Many times, expulsions are looked at as a permanent solution, but in reality, students may return to school in a few months and still have the same underlying wounds resulting in the same negative behaviors.

Increase Student Self-Esteem

The fifth reason why we should address wounded children is to increase their self-esteem that has been so heavily damaged. High self-esteem is extremely crucial to success in the classroom. The idea of building esteem could in itself take up a whole training session or book. As stated throughout the book, wounded children need to know that we are invested in them regardless of their past or current behavior. Nothing could be worse for our students than saying to them that I will let someone else deal with you and your behavior. It says to them that they are not worth our time or energy even though nothing could be further from the truth.

There will be times that their problems will be bigger than our knowledge base. In these cases, we must get someone who is more experienced in the area, such as a guidance counselor, administrator, or a trained professional. It is important, however, that we walk right along side them as they move through this process. Let them know that you are getting someone who can assist them because you care about them. Allow them to be a part of the process as well, so they feel they have some control.

There are times that some of us have conditions in which we will help someone. For instance, they have to be willing to help themselves first. With wounded children, we cannot make those kinds of conditions because many of them do not know how to help themselves. They will eventually need to take ownership of their behavior, but we cannot put conditions on them. Let them know that their behavior is what needs to change, not that they may or may not be welcome with that behavior. Rebuilding self-esteem is essential to classroom success as well as success later on in the student's life. They must feel like they have something of value to contribute to society and realize that they can overcome whatever emotional wounds they have suffered in the past.

Increase Student Emotional Quotient (EQ)

The sixth reason to address wounded children is to increase the student's emotional quotient (EQ). The latest research shows that our EQ can play a bigger role in our success in life than our IQ. This is because our EQ is the key tool to getting along with others, taking control of our life, thinking clearly, and making good decisions (Redenbach, 2004).

A student who is wounded has shut down on some emotional level, and it is critical that we pay attention to this. This is not a problem because we do not care, it is a problem because we have not had the training that teaches us how to care for our students' overall needs. How we get students to manage their emotions leads to a greater sense of self-esteem and ownership in their choices. When students have a greater sense of emotional health, learning and achievement take on a greater role in their life.

Increase Employment and Decrease Prison Rates

The seventh and eighth reasons to address wounded children are to increase chances of employment and decrease the chances of ending up in prison. According to Alliance for Education (n.d.-a), dropouts from the class of 2007 will cost the nation more than $329 billion in lost income over their lifetime. This goes to show the overall effect that employment has on our economy.

Though not all dropouts commit crimes or end up in jail or prison, dropping out does have an overall effect on finance and quality of life.

- ♦ Nearly one third of all public high school students— and nearly one half of all African Americans, Hispanics, and Native Americans—fail to graduate from public high school with their class. Of those who do graduate, only half have the skills they need to succeed in college or work.

- ♦ Dropouts are more than eight times as likely to be in jail or prison than a high school graduate.

- ♦ Dropouts earn $9,200 less per year than high school graduates and about $1 million less over a lifetime than college graduates (Silent Epidemic, n.d.).

Becoming the Resident Expert on Addressing the Wounded Student

As educators we must understand why we are doing what it is we are doing. The information in this chapter can seem overwhelming because the problem is so large, but it can serve as a guideline for you as you take a look at your school's policies and procedures and rules and regulations. I hope you feel empowered to stand up for the students in our schools who need our assistance. As teachers we have a strong voice of leadership. I encourage you to take this information to your school board as they set policies and procedures.

Compile the current information from your own school district regarding dropout, attendance, and overall student achievement and keep this research in mind when dealing with wounded children in your school. If your research shows that those issues are being addressed, see what you can do to increase those already high graduation and attendance rates. If your whole district is doing well, become a leader for other districts in your area or state that may be struggling in these areas.

If your district is struggling in some of the areas in this chapter, ask your administrator and school board for permission to establish the professional development team and training needed to address these issues. If we continue to do the wrong things with wounded students, we will continue to lose them. The dropout problem will continue to escalate unless extensive training and knowledge is gained from everyone in the school system. The wounded students are counting on you to take the lead and change the thinking about this topic in your school system.

The reason this is critical is because so many of us in today's schools wait for the expert to come in and tell us what to do or how it should be done. Though that training and gaining of new information is vital to create change, the change that needs to take place within your school system can only happen if you take that new information and apply it to the culture of your school and community.

Remember that each school culture and community is different, and what works at one school may not work at another. That is why it is difficult to bring someone in from the outside to build programs for your school district. The person from the outside can supply the content and structure for you to work on the issues at hand, but it is up to you to modify what they are saying based on your community. You have to become the resident expert. You must be willing to assume that role.

I have seen some teachers who have a very hard time in the role of expert in the field of education. We believe we are experts in our content. But, beyond that, some teachers do not have the confidence required in themselves or in the professional education of our children. It goes too far beyond the content area to help the whole child. That is why every teacher on his or her evaluation has a place for not just knowledge of content, but also of things like classroom management (i.e., can you understand your students enough to manage them).

I have found that many teachers have a wonderful ability to manage their students because of their ability to understand them and help them. Why do our teachers not mentor other teachers who may be struggling in classroom management? This would be a great opportunity to share the skills and knowledge they have about students. You can become the expert and help other teachers in your system develop new skills and understanding.

As a principal, I would have weekly staff meetings where I expected my teachers to fill me in on their ideas, training, or programs they were creating to help the students. What I found were some teachers who were apprehensive to make decisions—they were unsure of their ability to get creative on behalf of student learning. I would explain to them that I needed them to become the experts in the building on student achievement and student behavior. The response they always came back with bothered me on many different levels. They would say, just tell us what to do and we will do it. I truly did appreciate their trust in me and respect for my position, but that is not why I was there. I was there to allow them to be creative as well as to teach their students to do the same. This went on for several meetings before I finally had to say that I needed them to really use their schooling, training, years of experience, and expertise to help their children. I needed them to do this for the success of the students.

Somewhere in our education system I believe some teachers have lost the confidence in their own ability to make a difference. Teachers need to be proud of what they do for the children in our society and also be willing to help others who work with wounded children in and out of the school system. We now know why we must address wounded students. It is critical that you are the expert and that you take the lead in this area. Remember, wounded students may not make it without you.

The Bottom Line

The needs of today's students are complex and it is difficult to try to figure out viable solutions that work in every situation. By creating professional development learning opportunities for teachers in this area, we may avoid just suspending and expelling students we sometimes fail to understand.

A greater understanding of our students can lead to an increase in our overall attendance and graduation rate.

Chapter 4 Key Points

Why address wounded students?

+ Academic achievement;
+ Increase student attendance;
+ Decrease student dropout rates;
+ Decrease suspensions and expulsions;
+ Increase student self-esteem;
+ Increase student emotional quotient (EQ);
+ Increase employment rates; and
+ Decrease prison rates.

Use your years experience, schooling, and training to help others gain an understanding of wounded students in your district.

5

Addressing the Wounded Student

Programs That Promote Success for All Students

"Example teaches better than precept. It is the best modeler of the character of men and women. To set a lofty example is the richest bequest a man can leave behind him"
~ S. Mills, American Writer

The number one way to address the wounded student is to change the culture in our schools regarding how we view and administer discipline. There are many ways in which to view your school's discipline policy. Most policy views are set by social and school norms that have been in place for 30 years. They can be punitive and nontherapeutic in nature. Some might say it is not our job to be a therapist. This may be correct, but it is our job to be a teacher. William Glasser (2006) said it best, "Effective teaching may be the hardest job there is." We knew going in that the profession would be very difficult, but we also knew it would be rewarding. It is filled with no absolutes because we are working with the human condition. Walk into your neighborhoods, your churches, and your places of business and you will not only see, but perhaps accept, diversity and the human condition. Traditionally, our schools have not embraced differences in student behaviors and what may cause them. We say student discipline guidelines must be enforced with no exceptions so that we do not play favorites and so that students learn that punishment is swift and consistent for all behavior issues.

When I was introduced to the teachers during the first staff meeting of my first principal position, I asked them what they expect from a new principal. They had chosen a spokesman for the group as if they had been anticipating the question all along. He was a veteran coach. He stood up, saying "We expect the students to fear you and fear the office. Basically, get in their faces. These students need to understand who is in charge of this building." My first thought was, *don't we have an antibullying policy?* Instead, I said, "In that case, your school board and superintendent has just hired the wrong principal. I do not operate from a position of ego and control, but from a position of teaching and learning. When a student ends up in my office, he or she needs to learn and I am to teach or he will be back again and again. Consequences rarely ever result in changed behavior."

During the first situation at the school, the math teacher sent down a 17-year-old young man. While I was working, the young man walked into my office and admitted, "I just got sent down by Mr. Jones for calling him a name. What are you going to do to me?" Saying nothing, I ignored him as he continued to ask me the same question until finally, I broke into teaching, not punishing, mode.

"Young man, have you been taught the difference between right and wrong?"

"Yes."

"Was what you did right or wrong?"

"Wrong."

"Do you need another man to solve your problems?"

"No."

"Go solve your problem."

A few minutes later I saw the math teacher coming down the hall toward me and he said, "What did you do to that student? Did you get in his face and threaten him with the handbook and suspension? I have been teaching in this building for 26 years and I have never had a student apologize."

Teaching and giving responsibility where it belongs is necessary. Had I suspended the young man, which was under my control according to all the rules, guidelines, board policy, and laws, he would have learned nothing more than another lesson of failure and control. I will say that the young man did make the correct choice to do the right thing and apologize to the teacher. The student could have refused to make his comments right with the teacher and then a suspension might have been in order to create some distance so emotions could calm down.

The Steps to Addressing the Wounded Student

The way to address the wounded student is grounded in our commitment to change and our ability to see the big picture. Remember, every behavior is a chance to esteem or turn away a wounded student and every behavior is a teachable moment. In previous chapters you have learned how to understand and identify the wounded student, now you will learn how to address the wounded student. It is my goal to give you practical programs that you can use in your school to make a difference.

Do NOT Turn Over Your Power During a Teachable Moment

I see some teachers, administrators, and school employees who continuously turn their power over to someone else during a teachable moment. Many times it is turned over to someone who may not have as good an answer as you do or someone with less experience to draw on in order to help this student. We sometimes turn this power over because we are afraid that we will be held responsible for making a wrong decision. It is always good to use our school handbooks and policies to help guide us in making decisions; however, just like in parenting, there is no real handbook that says, *if you do this, go to point B and do this and all will turn out well.* Sometimes our inability to make decisions or lack of willingness to make a decision can be even more damaging to a wounded child.

This is not to say that students will not struggle or have learning difficulties. In fact, it is quite the opposite. This says that despite any obstacle that gets in the way of learning, we will overcome that obstacle and achieve. Our schools should be viewed as the one place in our community where each and every child will achieve their full potential. We can accomplish this lofty goal of achievement by starting with us and what we set as standards for our students.

One approach is to develop a "No-Failure School." Many wounded students who attend alternative schools or at-risk schools will tell you that they will get an F because that is what they are used to. It is ingrained into their belief system and the sooner they get their F, the sooner they can prove themselves right. Their belief system is destructive to their success. As many of you would guess, it is really not about whether they have the ability to pass their class or state required tests. It is more about their organization skills, test preparation, and the relevancy of the material to their complicated lives. When you throw their belief system of failure into the mix, you spell academic disaster.

Change the Way You Grade

The next step in addressing wounded students is by changing the way we traditionally grade in education. This is especially important when working with wounded children. We must try to get away from making finalizations or deadlines to achievement. Instead, we could use incompletes to mark progress. For many students put out of school on suspension, it is more about their behavior and not about their potential to achieve. An incomplete allows the student to feel like he/she still has the ability to accomplish something. It says to the student, "We have not given up on you." It assures the student that we believe he or she has the ability to learn the material. However, it is important to teach students that responsibility, deadlines, and ability in comprehension all have rewards and consequences in the real world.

We do not want to lose these students before the lesson is taught. Many wounded students have not learned this concept of responsibility at home, so the schools may be the only hope for the student to learn this lesson. I worked with a young lady who was pregnant and succeeding in her classes, but the baby came early in the month of May during the last month of school. At that point, because it had nothing to do with her ability to learn or try, we were able to give her an incomplete grade. In the fall, she was able to pick up where she left off and therefore completed her work and grades. If we had decided to fail her, it would have been perceived as a failure. She was not a failure simply because her child was born early.

Some educators have a hard time with this concept because we are very structured, highly motivated learners who, for the most part, established those skills earlier in our lives due to our upbringing. The first question that many of us asked in school was, "Where is the syllabus?" If we can see what is expected, we can start to plan our attack to accomplish the goals set forth by the teacher, and we could structure our time accordingly. Wounded children have a hard time structuring their time, and it is our job to help them acquire this skill. The best way to help wounded students is to establish relationships that are grounded in the fact that they can and will achieve. DO NOT set up barriers, like policies that say failure is a possibility. It is our job to teach them, and in some cases their failure is more a reflection of our failure than the students'.

As we move toward reaching a student's wounds, it is important to keep in mind that true change happens for most people on the emotional level and not on the cognitive level. That is why relationships that establish trust in your students' ability to achieve are so critical to this process.

A large issue that I had as a school administrator was that many policies in the typical handbooks require that teachers give Fs after so many unexcused absences. A suspension is usually counted as an unexcused absence. Many times, once a student has returned from a suspension, the failure for the grading period has already been determined. How do we expect unmotivated students, who already have a history of failing, to come back from a suspension and sit, let alone try, in a class that they literally have absolutely no chance of passing? We can say they should be there because it's required or just for the sake of learning, but we know this may not work.

This is one reason why alternative discipline is so important. This allows students to remain in the classroom and academically achieve. The consequences can be served in an alternative setting. We will discuss a specific program in chapter 6 that will help increase attendance and graduation while lowering suspension, dropout, and failure rates.

Take the Time to Train Your Staff

The third step to addressing wounded students is developing staff training. This sounds like a no-brainer. Realistically, how many of you have been to staff training where you have walked away either not gathering any new information as an educator, or you just simply are hearing the *same old, same old*? As stated before in the book, I know many of you care deeply for all children in your classroom and want to help, but unless you develop new, specific programs and policies to put in place, you will continue to see the same results. Give yourself the permission to think outside the box and dream big for your students.

Staff training when working with wounded students relies heavily on de-escalation skills and not on discipline techniques to change behavior. What we tend to see is that schools will try to strong-arm these behaviors with more security in case these students get out of hand. Again, I am not against safety or making schools a safe learning environment for teachers and students. In fact, de-escalation skills and training makes schools a much safer place for everyone emotionally and physically. Teaching people to understand wounded children and in de-escalation skills requires a new way of thinking and approach to a situation.

My karate instructor Larry Overholt was a career law enforcement officer for more than 30 years. He always told us that he never used his karate physically in a situation at work to intentionally harm anyone, but he did use it mentally in almost every situation because of its de-escalation techniques. Culturally, we train our officers and those who work in correctional facilities these skills, but no one teaches our educators. Why not? These skills can be of great benefit to us and our students to keep us all safer.

Personally, I believe this lack of training comes from our inability to change our mindset that a person must meet force with force. A place and time exists where this philosophy may be required, but the fact is last year in our public schools 1,511 students were corporally punished (Children's Defense Fund, 2008a). This stat reflects that we have a tendency to punish instead of de-escalate. If we work to ensure proper training to all of our educators, I believe we can eliminate many of these issues.

Perhaps the biggest question is whether to give staff training in the area of addressing wounded children. First, ask yourselves, "Is our current plan working?" If it is, I suggest you stick with your successful plan/program. On the other hand, if the answer is no, then seek information in this area. The responses

I have received as a public speaker, trainer, and staff developer in addressing wounded children have been overwhelming and shocking. The response has been consistent across the United States where I have spoken in Las Vegas, New Orleans, Michigan, Ohio, Tennessee, Florida, Texas, and Denver. From elementary to secondary conferences, everyone is saying the same thing: We need to have a clearer understanding of these children and programs that work to help them. It is my hope that this book will provide a way to better serve wounded children by sharing programs that will help transform the way we position our profession to help children who are struggling to receive their education. And to do this well, I believe we need workshops, staff training, and professional growth in de-escalation skills. I would suggest contacting your local law enforcement department, children's services, or social service agencies who may be able to provide this type of training. Counselors in your school may also have the training or contacts to get the staff training.

Increase Self-Esteem

The fourth way to address wounded students is to form programs that increase self-esteem. As you will see in chapter 6, where the components of self-esteem are described in detail, it is important to realize that the wounded student's self-esteem has been shattered. Understanding the effects of low self-esteem and how it is tied to achievement is critical to reaching the student. Remember that some students are coming from home lives that say they are worthless They are abused mentally and physically, and they come from a life of poverty and, the prevalent factor of low self-esteem, neglect. When a child feels neglected and unloved it damages their self-esteem more than anything else. Keeping in mind that the major influence on a child is the parent, good or bad, we can see why some children come to us with low to no self-esteem.

Every 36 seconds a case of child abuse or neglect is confirmed (Children's Defense Fund, 2008b). As horrible as this statistic is, this it is just the confirmed cases. Think of all the abuse and neglect that is not reported or that cannot be substantiated. This is not a small subject. This alone could become an entire staff training or book unto itself. How do we begin to deal with this type of figure and still educate these children? Some will argue that student achievement alone in the classroom will start to change this esteem issue. I agree that education plays a major part in helping to reach wounded children, but much needs to be done in the area of esteem building to prepare these students to learn again.

Counseling and Emotional Healing

With the current standard throughout schools, testing and data collection is demanding a lot from our school counselors' time. This means that the counseling time that our students need to succeed is lost to time spent on testing. Academic guidance counseling and testing is an important part of the educational process and cannot be ignored. However, our counselors do not have the time required to help wounded students reach the emotional level that they need to reach. In addition, the training really needed to assist these students is not usually offered to our counselors. To bring this to the forefront, our schools need to offer this as part of their counseling or have direct lines to get wounded children the specific help they need to be reached emotionally. We can then have plans in place to help them academically.

Here are some steps that can be general guidelines for you as a teacher when helping to reach wounded children:

Acknowledge: The first step to reaching a wounded student is to first acknowledge the wound. We are a society of stuffers who say *suck it up* or *pull yourself up by your own bootstraps*. These are all okay statements for the future once support and time are established, but they are not appropriate at the point of the original trauma. Many students will say that they are all right just because it is too painful to deal with the truth of the wounds in their lives. We must either be properly trained or have trained people on our staff to help us appropriately deal with these issues. If we do not acknowledge that our students are living complicated lives filled with pain, fear, anxiety, and trauma, then we may fail them.

Understand: The second step is to understand the student's wounds. I have stressed understanding a lot in this chapter because it is the key to proper care and reaching wounded children. Understanding our students' wounds means helping them bring the pain, along with its location, to light. If we plan to treat these wounds or get them to the correct resource, we must understand where the pain is coming from. Is it an abusive past? Or drugs? For us to help reach them, we must find the origin of the pain and try to understand it. Attempting to treat another wound instead of the one that really exists can be damaging to the student.

Relationship: The third step is taking the time to build a relationship with the student. This should come as no surprise to us. Who do we confide in when trouble surrounds us? We confide in people with whom we have the closest relationships; we trust them. Yet again this becomes a major issue today with educators because of time. When do we have time to develop relationships? We must find the time because of its importance in reaching wounded children. It is key to building relationships. If a child at home was in need, we would make that relationship with our own child our highest priority. Without time, how do we teach our child? It is a matter of priority and necessity. I have been to many schools that realize that they need to find ways in their schedule to support this kind of time. Each school will vary based on many issues. But the core of it all is that you must make the time. If our students realize we do not have time for them, it will only further feed their wounds of unintentional neglect and worthlessness.

Reaching wounded children: The fourth step is reaching the student's wounds and addressing them properly through professional care. This can be very cleansing for the student. Remember what we stated earlier, that all wounds must be brought to the surface to create healing. Wounds that stay unattended and are not surfaced will eventually get worse, like any deep flesh wound. These wounds can even start to manifest themselves into other wounds or problems.

Hope: The fifth step to reaching a wounded student is hope. Reaching the student's emotional needs leads to hope. Many wounded students have lost hope at a young age and your ability to teach or to be a great teacher has no meaning for a child who has lost hope. Once steps one through four have taken place, students will begin to see some hope and learning will start to have relevance. Learning needs to make sense to everyone. Hope has been discussed throughout this book and will continue to be discussed; it is the entire essence of this book.

Self-Esteem: The sixth step, self-esteem, can be broken down into four components as described by Clemes and Bean: connectiveness, uniqueness, empowerment, and models (Study on Self-Esteem as cited by Redenbach, 2004, p. 32). When wounded students begin to develop the four components of self-esteem, you will start to see a higher attentiveness to their schoolwork and academic success. We know that low self-esteem could lead to depression, lying, multiple behavior issues, even drugs. Self-esteem is one of the building blocks to reaching the wounds of students that is probably the most critical to the human spirit in restoring hope.

Connectiveness: Everyone wants to feel connected to something else or something bigger than themselves. Many wounded students feel disconnected from people or organizations such as schools. We all want a sense of belonging, no matter what our age.

Uniqueness: Acknowledging unique qualities gives your students a sense of identity. In our schools, sometimes we punish students subconsciously for being different. Some rules are designed for conformity. A certain sense of conformity is definitely needed for safety and consistency for all. But we take it sometimes to a point where students lose their own style, and this can affect their style of learning as well. Students need to feel unique. They may express themselves through art, music, and sports, but they can sometimes lose that sense of expression in the formal classroom.

Empowerment: Empowering students gives them a sense of control. When students or children in general lash out at others through things such as bullying, fighting, or worse types of violence, it is ultimately a sense of regaining power or a way to gain some type of control.

Models: It is also critical to model behaviors we want students to pick up on. Having someone's values to model that are acceptable in our schools and in society plays a major role in esteem building. Again, as stated earlier, parents are not always present or do not set the proper model for their child's behavior. The teacher then becomes the next powerful model in a child's life. To model a positive outlook on life alone can be a total change to a wounded child's beliefs. Compassion, hope, and grace are all behaviors that some children have never been exposed to and may never get the chance again to be exposed to beyond the teacher. It is important to understand that self-esteem will eventually lead to self-control and self-control to self-discipline which can lead to a whole new area in which most students who are wounded have never been, and that is hope.

The Bottom Line

I believe the whole message behind working with wounded children is our ability as teachers to extend grace, mercy, and forgiveness to the children we are working with. I have had several questions and concerns in this area regarding what we are really teaching students if we give them breaks. Some people have even replied to me that the world is cruel, and giving wounded children a little grace and mercy just sets them up for future failure. "That's the problem with kids today: they are just given too many breaks." My response to this is: If you have ever had or will ever have any level of wounds, how would you want people to respond to you?

If you are picked up by the police for speeding, would you roll down your window and say to the officer, "I deserve the full punishment for this offense. If it requires the maximum fine, even jail time, I will take it so that I can learn my lesson that the world is a cruel place and this way it will never happen again." In my opinion, the majority of us would roll down that window and hope for some grace, mercy, and maybe a little forgiveness from the officer enforcing the law. Grace is defined as disposition to or an act or instance of kindness, courtesy, or clemency, a temporary exemption (Merriam-Webster Online Dictionary, 2008). How many of us have needed a temporary exemption from something at some point in our lives? I know that I have, and the people in my life who have applied that grace and mercy have become some of my greatest teachers because they built a trusting relationship that feels safe to learn under.

We have to keep the main thing the main thing, and that is student achievement. I encourage you to use this with your students. If you apply some of these rules to your classroom instead of punishment and consequences, you will begin to see student success increase. Students will feel safe and know that it is okay to be human.

Chapter 5 Key Points

- ◆ Consequences rarely result in changed behavior.
- ◆ Never turn your power over during a teachable moment.
- ◆ Every behavior is a teachable moment.
- ◆ Develop staff training regarding wounded students.
- ◆ Develop de-escalation skills.
- ◆ Develop self-esteem programs for students.
- ◆ Have trained professional staff in place to help wounded students.

6

Self-Esteem and the Wounded Student

Making the Shift: Dealing With Behaviors

"I am not concerned that you have fallen; I am concerned that you arise."
~ Abraham Lincoln, Sixteenth President

The number one thing that people want me to explain during my seminars is the definition of *wounded*. At first I was not sure exactly what they were asking. I thought that the word spoke for itself. But what I finally realized was that for educators this is a new term in the field. When I speak with counselors, pastors, or therapists this term is in their field of practice and a part of why their clients go to see them. But for educators, we do not necessarily assume that this will be something that we will be dealing with. So for some of us, it remains outside our scope of research and training.

The Components of Good Teaching

Before we get to defining the term *wounded*, it is important to again emphasize exactly what good teaching is. I do not want to suggest that we are not good teachers or that we are not trying or have not had the proper training. In an article written by Marshall Brain (1998), he describes good teaching in four key components:

1. **"Knowledge of the subject."** As a public school administrator, almost everyone I would interview for academic positions came into their interviews on a level playing field in this area. Having graduated from college with a degree in an area of specialty, everyone has a certain level of knowledge that makes them all close to equal.

2. **"The ability to convey that knowledge."** This brings us to a key word: *communication*. Are you a great communicator of the knowledge you possess? Can you teach your students the material and teach them to problem solve to get answers that apply to what you are teaching. The area of guided discovery is extremely important in effective teaching. Can you get your students to a level of mastery?

3. **"Interest."** Good teachers can get their students to want to learn the material because it is fun, exciting, and most importantly, relevant to their lives and the world around them. This is

where the separation occurs between good teaching and bad. According to the High School Survey of Student Engagement (Yazzie-Mintz, 2006) which surveyed 81,499 students in 110 schools within 26 different states, two out of three students claim they are bored in class in high school at least every day; 17% of the respondents are bored in every class in high school. Only 2% of the students surveyed have never been bored in high school. The study which was done by the Center for Education Evaluation and Education Policy and Indiana University School of Education, goes on to say that, three out of four students state that the reason they are bored in class is that "material wasn't interesting," and 39% state that "material wasn't relevant to me." And 31% of the respondents indicate they are bored in class because they have "no interaction with teacher." Another example for elementary school teachers, the National Institute of Health, one of the largest studies in U.S. classrooms today, states that our fifth graders spent 91.2% of class time in their seats listening to the teacher or working alone. Furthermore, only 7% of students work in small groups which fosters critical thinking and social skills, as stated by Toppo (2007) in *USA Today*. Clearly, research is crucial if we are to go in a direction that has relevance to our students.

4. "Respect of the students." Here is the one aspect of an interview that would start to separate candidates for the school climate I wanted to create for my students. Can the teacher respect and understand where all students are coming from educationally, emotionally, and physically? We all live and are trained in a world of hardware, but our students are not hardware. In fact, they are software. Each brain that enters the classroom is its own computer ready to be programmed by you, the teacher.

Some of the software programs that enter your classroom on a daily basis have already been programmed with viruses that are hard to break through. Sometimes these viruses override the previous four qualities you possess as a teacher. You are knowledgeable in your subject area, so take that and use it to create lessons that are engaging and relevant to your students' lives. Unfortunately, that virus can be hard to overcome because it was programmed before we got the students in our classroom.

The question for us is: can we or do we now have the skills as teachers to override that virus and reprogram students who want to learn? Have we restored hope, relevance, excitement, dreams, and goals to their lives? Have we told them that their lives count today? If so, they will believe their lives count even more because of their new sense of purpose.

What it Means to be Wounded

Thus far in this chapter we have discussed research from elementary and high school levels that supports the idea that something is missing, that there can sometimes be a disconnection between teacher and student. This disconnection stems from our misunderstanding of the word *wounded* and how it affects the children we are teaching and how it affects the environment of our classrooms.

What does it mean to be wounded? Look at the definitions (www.dictionary.com, n.d.) below and see if any of these terms apply to the students in your classroom.

1. **Suffering**: Are any of your students suffering?
2. **Injured**: Have some of the students in your classroom been injured, perhaps physically, or perhaps in another form?
3. **Marred**, **impaired**, or **damaged:** Do any of these terms apply to any of your students?

When I think of the thousands of children who I have worked with over the years, all of these words do apply to many wounded students. I can add more: scared, worried, unsure, insecure, angry, hurt, and pained. How do you define some of your students?

For years we have looked at these students as at-risk, and consequently we have made at-risk programs designed to help at-risk children. Do you see again the disconnection between our students and learning? In my opinion, we have given a wrong diagnosis to some students and then given wrong treatments. Again, I believe that we do have children who are at-risk, and programs and research do help students who fit that diagnosis. We need to continue looking at ways to support all of our students and provide what we can to assist them. This can be difficult for many districts that are cutting costs and losing good services that have been around to assist children for years in their district. This further demonstrates our need to try to get our teachers the best professional training to help all students academically, socially, and emotionally.

The Difference Between At-Risk and Wounded

The behaviors at-risk and wounded children exhibit are different in many ways. When attempting to distinguish between these two types of children, again the first question you should ask the child is: What are your hopes and dreams? For the majority, a student who is at-risk can still answer this question and think about possibilities for his or her future. Sometimes for an at-risk student those hopes or dreams need to be guided into a more positive light so that those goals can be constructively achieved. For instance, an at-risk student might say that he would like to make plenty of money so that he can provide for his family. A reasonable goal, but as many of us know, there are many ways to be rich or gain wealth. Therefore, the ability to channel this goal through hard work, sacrifice, and education could be a different thought than what this student originally had in mind.

Wounded children, on the other hand, have in many ways given up on themselves and others. They are so busy dealing with their painful past or just surviving that today does not really allow much time for dreaming or being hopeful for a brighter future. They are so defeated by life that they are just making it through today. When a student lacks these hopes and dreams, it is imperative that they are restored before learning can take place or be relevant and make sense. The disconnection is the source of much of the frustration we feel as teachers. The good news is that we can become educated in dealing with wounded children and start to reconnect with these children and their emotional needs. Students in your classroom are highly emotional beings, and we need to use these emotions to their advantage.

This is not to say that we need to forget about content, setting realistic goals through proper lesson plans, testing, or even classroom discipline. Remember, learning needs to make sense and be relevant. We need to deal with the fact that the wounded children in our classrooms may not see our material as relevant to their lives despite how well prepared and knowledgeable you are as the teacher. Ralph Waldo Emerson (2006) supported this very idea when he said, "the secret of education lies in respecting the pupil."

Discipline, Not Punishment

We must make the shift as educators on how we look at behaviors in our classroom and what our students are saying to us. No way should we ignore negative behaviors, especially at the cost of safety or the interference of the learning of others. Thankfully, like the at-risk programs, we can set up programs in which wounded children can receive the proper discipline that does not demean, embarrass, or judge them. The word *discipline* means to train or teach. The term *punishment* does not come into the picture when teaching. If a student commits an offense that requires assistance outside of your classroom, then let justice be served for those more severe behaviors. The good news is that we do not have to be the implementers of that justice or be the judge.

An important point to also keep in mind, even when dealing with students who are being expelled for major offenses, is that these students will return to your school despite a lengthy expulsion. Even worse, they may return with a vengeance or more anger, adding on top of that the fact that they are now far behind in their education. However, they could also return with hope. What kind of program does your school have for your expelled students both during and after their expulsion? Is a lesson being learned regarding their unacceptable behavior? Will they instead make the conclusion that no one wants to teach them, or does the expulsion just reinforce their opinion of themselves as being worthless, therefore forcing them into isolation again?

We cannot let these teachable moments escape us. Where do you learn your greatest life lessons? Usually they are learned in the ditch of life, rarely on the smooth road. I suggest implementing programs to work with students during their expulsions. I have seen programs that were offered off campus and staffed by a certified teacher and teacher's aid. One example of this type of program was an online computer series that allowed students to keep up academically and work on the behaviors that previously led them to their current state.

The key behind a program like this one is having a staff that is well trained in working with wounded children as well as curriculum. Over a 3 year period, the teachers were able to take on 20 students who were expelled, and 19 of those students ended up graduating on time and did not return to the program. The greatest strength of the staff is that they knew who their students were and treated them with respect, giving them a sense of hope to recover from their unwise decisions.

Many of these decisions were based on their wounds. The program provided counseling individually and in groups. It also had a strong intake process that required parent involvement from the very beginning. I am not suggesting that everything always went smoothly. A great deal of understanding and work on every individual's part was necessary for success. Everyone had to find the wound inside of these students, get them to the surface and then deal with it head on. Each situation was unique and carried its own set of issues to get past for the growth of the student into the healing process. What we saw in the end was a student who had restored confidence and a new sense of purpose for his or her life. The program involved community agencies as support services, as well as a mentoring program for the students involved.

The "Serve" Program

Another program that can be used to help you reduce suspensions, decrease dropouts, and increase achievement and the graduation rate is the "Serve" program. After training the staff of its importance to the school climate and academic achievement, schools have experienced amazing outcomes. During the 3 years of my career in my most recent school, we lost only three students to expulsion. The school superintendent informed me that before the program was installed, he was receiving about 20 angry parent phone calls a month because students were being thrown out of school at a record pace. This was not the result of a lack of caring in the teachers or administrators, but instead stemmed from their lack of proper training to deal with their wounded students' behaviors. After the "Serve" program was implemented, the superintendent said he went from 20 to zero complaints in those 3 years. The "Serve" program has been used by other schools that have had similarly exciting results.

This program is extremely east to start; the only catch is that it requires a whole new way of thinking about discipline. It really begins with a mission and vision statement that simply states that in order for academic achievement to take place, students need to be in a seat and discipline (teaching behaviors) will take place during nonacademic time. This program also allows everyone to be involved in the process, and it becomes a more consistent way of giving students what they really need to improve behavior: your time and expert teaching.

We as teachers arrived here because we have skills that allowed us to achieve a certain academic level. All educators can model what it takes to be a good student. Remember that teachers are the second biggest influence in a child's life, and in the absence of parents, we are the number one influence. We know much of what we do today through the modeling of our parents, grandparents, and past teachers.

How the "Serve" Program Works

The "Serve" program will take place before or after school and will be an alternative to school suspensions. Suspensions are not always a meaningful teaching tool in education. If and when a negative behavior occurs, some teachers have been trained to banish students to the office, expecting the administration to suspend them. Anything less is considered a victory on the student's behalf, leaving the teacher feeling defeated and unsupported. Our school discipline procedures often present little more than an "us against them" mentality. To change a person from the inside, it is best to use modeling and teaching rather than consequences. This program is designed to do just that.

It should be viewed as an intervention to get students back on track and into their seats as soon as possible so that curriculum can be taught. After serving as a teacher for 10 years, as well as a school administrator for 11, I can assure you that the systems that many schools use today are not of benefit to anyone. Teachers, administrators, and students all lose. Teachers cannot get students to achieve because they lose them from their classroom, and students lose because they continue to get further and further behind, and the administration loses because they want to keep suspensions to a minimum to keep students on track academically.

The "Serve" program puts the teachers in direct contact with the students in order to resolve the behavior while the administrator acts only as a support or a mediator in the process. Let me give a specific example of what it could look like. A student's behavior is unacceptable in school policy; therefore the teacher gets a "Serve" paper (see below) and informs the student that he has the option of suspension or the "Serve" program before or after school hours. Obviously, you will decide the available time slots for the program if implemented into your school system. The "Serve" program usually runs for 2 hours. The first hour is devoted to teaching, learning, and an intervention regarding the student's behavior. For instance, if you have students in the

"Serve" Program

Student Name: _____ Date: _____ Grade: _____

Address: _____ Phone: _____

Assigning Teacher: _____

Behavior: _____

Outcome needed for student improvement: _____

Parent Contact: Date: _____ Time: _____ Phone: _____

Who called the parents? _____

Parent agreed to program: Yes ___ No ___

Date to be served: _____ Program Completed: Y ___ N ___

Student Signature: _____ Teacher: _____

Administration Signature: _____

"Serve" program who were caught smoking, they will discuss as a group the dangers of smoking with a teacher, administrator, or community agency.

The second hour is designed for students to perform meaningful services to the school with a staff member or community agency. These programs of service are designed to build esteem and instill school pride. Service tasks and chores like cleaning toilets or mopping floors are not acceptable. A staff member keeps a running list of what needs to be done in and around the school. Such services can include making bulletin boards in the cafeteria that are antismoking, helping to set up for school events, assisting a secretary or other staff with projects, and so on. This gives your staff a chance to work with these students in a positive manner and allows everyone the ability to offer their knowledge and skills to the students.

In order to build a healthy school environment, it is imperative that everyone on your staff is viewed as a teacher, and not just a snitch or tattler. If your school secretary sees unacceptable behavior from a student, then he or she should be encouraged to use that teachable moment. The same goes for cafeteria workers, custodians, and any school employee. The reasons that many wounded children are turned off by school is because they feel we are just another part of their lives that does not understand them, and in turn, care for them. As far as they are concerned, we do nothing more than pass them off like a problem. Think what would happen in your school if everyone from the superintendent on down were viewed as teachers who had time to deal with the behaviors that need to be dealt with in a swift but caring manner.

In the history of school discipline, most misbehavior is sent to the principal's office. I can speak from experience that with the number of office referrals, plus other duties, no principal can give exactly what each student needs to change behavior. And taking into account a teacher's work day, it is next to impossible for a teacher to give exactly what each student needs as well as work with 30 to 40 kids at a time. The program is designed to help alleviate some of that pressure from our teachers and administrators during the normal school day and allow them to set up programs that work well after school. A modified copy of the "Serve" form can be used to fit any special needs of your school.

There are times that the office is a necessary place for a period of time. I have seen better relationships develop between teacher and student if that teacher comes to the office when they are available to talk to their students once the space has been given for the student to calm down and the teacher does not have other students at the time needing attention. The "Serve" program can be used as a form of teaching that says to the student you can serve your time outside of class because for now you need to be in your seat and learning.

Giving a "Serve" paper to a student only requires that you talk to the student and call the parent or guardian in order to inform them that this program is in place of a suspension. If they refuse the "Serve" program, the suspension will take place. Over the years I have seen very few students and parents refuse the "Serve" program and choose suspension. This kind of communication is critical for relationship building and positive public relations with parents. This is why the parent complaints made to the superintendent's office decreased so significantly: the parents were a part of the process and liked the idea of teaching their child responsibility while keeping their child in school. Parents realize that school is a much safer place for any child, especially a child who has been wounded.

Keep it Simple

First of all, when developing a service program for your school, use the resources that you have in your community. We have had students spend time at the Humane Care Center or where they are working with others who may need assistance in the community, such as special needs children or the elderly. Being a service to others or your community can give wounded children an amazing sense of self worth and sense of belonging, thus building up their much needed self-esteem. Remember the four components of self-esteem: connectiveness, uniqueness, empowerment, and model. This program fits in directly at the heart of reaching wounded children. The possibilities to build esteem through this program are endless and cost very little to operate. The "Serve" program above started with a $1,000 grant and lasted 3 years. We just needed materials to complete some of the projects (paper for bulletin boards, markers, journals, educational materials, etc.).

The program is staffed by everyone. We ran the program on Tuesdays and Thursdays after school for 2 hours. The size of our staff only required that each staff member gave 2 days a year after school to the program. It is a voluntary staff program, but I found many staff members enjoyed the result and time with the students. The difference sometimes between the rules and the students is a relationship. Results overall for the program in a 3-year span included suspensions being cut in half, office referrals decreasing significantly, and academic achievement and graduation increased while drop outs decreased.

The "Serve" program is not designed to handle students who are breaking the law, threatening the safety of students, or interfering with the learning of students. These students should be handled by the school administrator. Issues such as drugs, weapons, or other safety concerns need to be dealt with immediately. The "Serve" program can deal with attendance issues, classroom discipline issues, minor infractions, dress code violations, first offenses, swearing, smoking, failure to complete homework assignments, skipping class, and so forth.

The "Serve" model is represented as such:

"Serve"

Wounded Children

Major Offense—No "Serve" Program Option	Minor School Offenses
Recommendation Expulsion	"Serve" Program Offered to Student/Parents
Possible Law Involvement	"Serve" Program
Offer a program once justice has been served. Establish your off-site expulsion program for expulsion students.	Student Returns to Class

The Bottom Line

It is important to keep in mind your mission and vision for all children in your school. Think about achievement and remember that the programs you offer students should reflect your priority to keep students in their seats, in a classroom, and ready to learn. Students should ideally only be removed from the classroom for long periods of time for issues like weapons, drugs, violence, constant disturbance, or keeping others from learning. Continue as well to build programs in your classroom and building that promote self-esteem. This is such a vital part to the process of healing.

One teacher developed a car wash for students who needed something constructive to do as a service project. They decided to wash cars for staff and the community and then give the money earned to charity. The students had to organize the car washes, get materials, and set up a particular system for success that required teamwork and organization. By the end of the fourth car wash, the students had raised more than $400 for charity. We had the local president of the charitable organization come to the school, and we asked the students to present her with the check. The local newspaper agreed to write an article on the students' charitable act of giving. This really allowed the students to focus outward to help others, which is a key part of reaching wounded students.

In the end, one student spoke to all of us about his newfound dream to grow up and do this for a living. Humored by his speech a student laughed, remarking, "You want to wash cars for a living?" "No," he said. "I want to help people." His remark really caught the attention of everyone present. Up to this point, this particular student had always been the focus of negative attention, always receiving and rarely giving. He appreciated the good feeling he received when he offered of himself: he gained a sense of worth.

Why did most of us go into teaching in the first place? Teaching rewards us with a sense of purpose through serving others. As teachers we can certainly understand why our students would feel the same way when giving to another. In my opinion, it should be in our job description to provide our students with such rewarding opportunities.

Chapter 6 Key Points

- ◆ Good teaching is: (1) knowledge of subject; (2) conveying that knowledge; (3) making it relevant and interesting; and (4) respecting your students.
- ◆ At-risk means that the student still has goals.
- ◆ Wounded students have given up on goals and dreams.
- ◆ Give meaningful discipline.
- ◆ Discipline means to train or teach.
- ◆ Use alternative discipline methods for teaching.
- ◆ Develop a "Serve" program to increase self-esteem and increase achievement.
- ◆ Components of self-esteem: connectiveness, uniqueness, empowerment, model.

7

Emotional Issues

Understanding the Stages of Behavior

*"People acting together as a group can accomplish things which
no individual acting alone could ever hope to bring about."*
~ Franklin D. Roosevelt, Thirty-Second President

Understanding behavior and what causes the varieties of behavior you experience in your classroom can become the largest obstacle in teaching. Let's start with the big picture. Today it is estimated that there are more than 143 million orphans in the world (Orphan's Hope, 2008). That is enough children to go three times around the equator. Every 18 seconds, another child becomes an orphan, without a mother or father. At any given point, there are more 500,000 children in the U.S. foster care system. Each year, an estimated 20,000 young people "age out" of foster care. Many are only 18 years old and still need support and services. Of those who "aged out" of foster care:

- 54% earned a high school diploma;
- 2% obtained a bachelor's degree or higher;
- 51% were unemployed;
- 30% had no health insurance;
- 25% had been homeless; and
- 3% were receiving public assistance (Shaohannah's Hope, 2006).

These numbers are staggering and could continue to grow. Many of these children are born with no sense of purpose or belonging. These are deep emotional wounds; these children suffer from a lack of connection from the beginning.

Collectively, we are a nation that boasts of having the most millionaires and billionaires of all 25 industrialized countries, but we are also ranked 18th in the percentage of children in poverty and 14th when considering our efforts to lift children from poverty, 23rd in infant mortality, and then last, 25 out of 25, for protecting our children against gun violence. Gun violence leads to community violence. Between 1979 and 2004, gunfire killed 101,413 children and teens in the U.S. (Children Defense Fund, 2004).

I can easily continue with statistics regarding children and their behaviors. The United States has a high divorce rate, leaving children with a home life that is falling apart. Of course, there are many single parents who do a wonderful job raising well-balanced, successful children in and out of the classroom. I have the greatest respect for those single parents who are able to balance all the necessary skills of raising healthy children. I have had some of those children in my classroom as well. I can also put in the equation how much grandparents contribute to the support of both two-parent and single-parent homes.

For some of us, we can understand where these students are coming from. For some of us, we cannot begin to understand. What we do know is that our students today are living in higher poverty, unstable homes, and feel unsafe about the world around them. We have to try to keep from judging their behaviors and try to understand to the best of our ability who our students are, why they behave this way, and what we can do to assist them.

This chapter targets behavior and the understanding of the stages of that behavior. Behaviors demonstrate that our students are hurting. Buried deep in their subconscious minds are turmoil, lies, destructive thoughts, self-fulfilling prophesies, and loads of dysfunction. As stated before, our students are emotional beings. Our students are living in an emotional state, dealing with wounds from their past as well as those they are trying to endure currently.

Stages of Emotions

Wounded: These students have emotional wounds including, but not limited to, neglect, abuse, anger and no/low self-esteem. These students do not have the ability to concentrate or stay on track during a traditional school day. They also lack communication skills and have difficulty with responsibility and cooperation. Behaviors and attitudes are severely affected.

Survival: These students do what it takes to get by. They can border between wounded or academic. They can be considered our at-risk students.

Academic: These students have the ability to think clearly and focus on their academic achievement as well as a career path.

As adults we try to surround ourselves with people with whom we have deep emotional ties. By doing this, we know that when we are hurting, we will have the support of loving family and friends. Unfortunately, many students do not have this support.

As adults, we ultimately take responsibility for our behaviors. Depending on many factors, it may take some of us longer than others, but the end result is still the same. It is critical for everyone to understand, students included, that we are all responsible for how we act in relation to how we think and feel.

Behaviors are either positive or negative in a verbal or physical way or they are passive in nature. The final stages of getting your students to turn the corner is getting them to listen. Our listening skills have been diminished due to the media and video games; people are not there to listen. The interactive conversations of an earlier age before the advancements in technology (e-mail, text messaging, and computers) no longer exist. We have instant conversations instead and it seems like too much work to actually find the time to converse personally. That's why some students are not being heard: they have lost the art of communication and find it hard to believe that anyone really would want to take the time to find out what they are really thinking and feeling.

When we do ask questions, we sometimes ask defensive questions, such as: Why didn't you turn in your work? Why did you behave that way? Why were you late to school? Try to stay away from the "why" questions, especially with wounded, and thus defensive, children. Take time and ask instead, "What is going on that made you late today? What is going on in your life to cause this behavior?" It really starts to open up the doors of communication. It says to your student: I have time and I am concerned with your life. In this way, the two-way, face-to-face communication starts to occur.

I have worked with thousands of students in juvenile lock-up facilities, alternative schools, and with inner city youth. In every one of these instances, when I worked with a student who I was concerned was wounded emotionally or physically, I would ask,

"What's going on?" It would end with the student responding with a difficult question for me to answer, such as, "What would you do?" or "What would you have done in my shoes?" This opens not just a conversation but an avenue to teaching and learning. Somewhere we feel like if students would just listen, then things would be much better in today's school system. The fact is that they will listen once we tap into that part of their emotional beings. The breakdown of communication is something that can cause a breakdown in almost any relationship.

Two other core concerns that were touched on in chapter 1 that can and most likely will destroy a relationship if given the opportunity are ego and control. A relationship is built on a partnership of trust, communication, and understanding. Personally, I just cannot simply say that if my wife would just listen, then our relationship would go more smoothly. This statement implies that I am right and that she is wrong without so much as a discussion. Nearly all relationships are 50/50, and the truth usually resides somewhere in the middle. At times we are put into positions as the decision maker, or authority figure, such as a teacher. The decision that we ultimately make needs to be respected by all those involved, students in this case, so we can *not* cut down or cut out our conversations.

Developing Programs for Wounded Students

We as human beings do not operate well in isolation. A person who is receiving the maximum penalty in prison is sometimes subjected to isolation. With this isolation, many inmates could start to develop severe emotional pain and mental problems. Although this is an extreme example, it does demonstrate the correlation between isolation and the human condition. As human beings we prefer and essentially need community or group support. We have to secure learning that engages and encourages cooperation, communication, team work, and responsibility.

We have the ability to develop programs for our wounded students that say we are willing to climb in the ditch with you and this school is a community center for listening, success, and hope. Usually, we talk about negative behavior or just behaviors in a negative light. Remember that many of our students have positive behaviors because they have had appropriate models, reinforcement, and feedback.

Teachers often ask what programs are available that will assist in improving their students' self worth, will engage their students, and will develop problem solving methods to help students think critically and take chances based on conversations and new information. I had a young lady at my high school who was smoking during school hours in the restroom. She had already served 3-, 5-, and 10-day suspensions. Expulsion was technically the only option left. Even though the girl deserved her consequences, the bottom line was that despite these consequences and discipline plan she was going to continue to smoke. I asked the student if she would attend anti-smoking classes held after school through a community agency in our district. I told her that if she agreed to attend these class sessions through completion, then I would withhold her expulsion. To gain some support from home, I involved her guardian in this process as well. Of course, her guardian was in favor of her remaining in school. I informed the student that if she completed the course successfully and would start the process of quitting smoking, then I could use her as a model for the rest of the students in the school who want to quit, or she could even encourage others to attend the community class.

This student was a junior when she chose this option to stay in school and she did complete the program and she did work with other students who where caught smoking in school. By her senior year, she was the vice president of the student council. This program changed her behavior because:

1. She obtained new information.
2. She felt connected to the school.
3. She modeled positive behavior instead of negative.
4. She was engaged in the process and took responsibility for her behavior.
5. She had choices and was taught problem-solving skills (critical thinking).

6. She was not isolated as a consequence, which could have caused further emotional damage.

On graduation day, this young lady told me that she was signed up for the military and she knew it was only possible because of her new-found confidence and self-worth; in addition, she was no longer smoking, therefore making basic training survivable.

Every behavior is a way in which wounded students are communicating with us. We must become better with nonverbal cues that students are throwing our way. We have to stop being intimidated, upset, or fearful of what they are saying and become the answer they are so desperately looking for. The major issue that needs to be kept in mind when working with wounded children and developing programs for students within your school is to look at the external systems in your community that will be happy to assist your students. In this case, we used an antismoking program that was already provided within our community. Many of your external agencies in your community can be the expert for some of your students' needs.

You can set up groups or individuals with some of the agencies. Some agencies services may have a cost and some may not. If money does become an issue for services for student programming, there are always grants to help with this. The idea is to provide opportunities of learning for your students that are not punitive in nature. And using as many resources as possible will make your job less stressful and provide you with some peace of mind that you are helping the child out with the best professional service possible.

Your ability to make connections and acquire outside resources will also help to lighten your heavy load. With the pressures of accountability at every turn and paper work and documentation demands getting higher and higher, the issues and problems we have to endure on a day-to-day basis are not easy or for the faint of heart. We need to make sure we take care of ourselves and not overextend into a state of burn out. When we do we are of no service to anyone—our families, our students, or our community.

At the core of every teacher is the desire to see all of his or her students take the next step academically and for them to leave the classroom a better person than when they entered. To get this out of every student is a difficult task to ask of anyone. You must take care of yourself physically and emotionally if you wish to care for the needs of others. Your strength will be needed as those months pass by.

Bullying in Schools

Another behavior that is prevalent in today's schools is bullying. There are several theories on what causes bullying. Some psychologists believe that bullies actually lack self-esteem and bully in order to boost their self-esteem. These bullies are often the victims of other bullies at home or school, so they act out on students at school to gain control of their self-worth. Others would say that bullies actually have high self-esteem. These bullies feel they have a sense of entitlement. Personally, I believe that many teachers who have been in the classroom long enough can see that many bullies fit both descriptions well.

From what I have discovered through my years of experience dealing with bullies and victims of bullying, certain traits do exist and it is the same trait in both groups, whether they have low or high self-esteem. According to Jane St. Clair (n.d.) in her article "What Causes Bullies?" they have contempt for the weak and view them as their prey. They lack empathy and foresight and do not accept responsibility for their actions. "Bullying is a learned behavior and not a character trait.... Researchers have not been able to find a link to any particular religion, race, income level, divorce or any other socioeconomic factor.... Just like wounded behaviors, it crosses all barriers." Also, it is important to realize that boys and girls can exhibit bullying behaviors, they just exhibit different behaviors and in different ways. Boys are likely to be physical bullies, while girls are verbal bullies.

There is a lot of information available about bullying. It is a huge issue in our schools as well as our society. According to *Bullying: Facts for Schools and Parents* (Cohn & Canter, 2003), bullying is the most common form of violence in our society: between 15 and 30% of students are bullies or victims. My thoughts are that as we implement some of the strategies about building self-esteem and addressing the emotional issues of our students in a positive manner, we will start to see a decrease in bullying in our schools.

A Model to Improve Bullying

1. Communication to parents and students on reporting bullying.
2. Keep parents informed of any problems that may exist in our school through meetings or letters.
3. As a staff, be visible in halls between classes, cafeteria, and after school. This can cut the problem almost in half.
4. Use community resources for prevention programs.
5. Make sure all school employees have been educated about the issue and how to handle those issues when they arise, such as de-escalation skills, reporting, and other intervention strategies.
6. Create an environment that says we are available and you are safe.

The good news about bullying is that it is a behavior that can change through education and intervention. Making antibullying policies that simply state "no bullying" will not change the behavior. We need to involve parents and programs that present bullying as an unacceptable behavior in school. We need to discuss with everyone involved that bullies can choose different, more positive ways to get the attention they are seeking.

The Bottom Line

The needs of our students are becoming increasingly complicated and require teachers today to have the proper training for how our students that are emotionally wounded will be acting out in school. We can be prepared by developing programs that will address those needs. Reaching out to our local agencies to access services is not only needed, it is necessary along with involving parents to the best of our ability. By understanding the emotional needs of our students and providing our teachers and administrators professional development in this area, we will begin to see improvement in our wounded students.

Chapter 7 Key Points

- ♦ Three stages of emotions: wounded, survival, academic.
- ♦ Emotions have a major effect on learning.
- ♦ Ask "what" and not "why" questions.
- ♦ Develop connections with local agencies to help with programs and understanding.
- ♦ Be visible and involve parents when developing antibullying campaigns.

8

Reaching the Wounded Student

Teachable Moments Result in Hope for All Students

"Character cannot be developed in ease and quiet. Only through experiences of trial and suffering can the soul be strengthened, vision cleared, ambition inspired and success achieved."

~ Helen Keller

Regardless of what position of life you are in, rich or poor, young or old, sick or healthy, we all need hope. For our wounded students, who are just surviving day to day, much if not all of their hope has been taken from them early on. It is part of our responsibility to restore the hope that will allow them to dream and believe in themselves and others again. Schools are places of learning. What greater gift can we give students than their hope and their education? The success for everyone in life relies on hope.

Over the past 2 years, I have been trying to give the best example I can in regard to just how important it is to help wounded children and what roles we play as educators in this process. I have given some thoughts, examples, and hopefully inspiration because I believe these students need their teachers in order to make it. During my last position as principal a few years ago, I talked to the staff about the difference between at-risk and wounded children. Many of them appreciated the proper identification of the difficulties they have in front of them with the children in their classrooms. They agreed that their students have issues that go beyond the at-risk tag.

The one person on my staff who served as my behavior intervention specialist for the students made a very interesting observation regarding the term *wounded* and his past experiences. He was a retired Marine sergeant of 20 years. He came up to me and said he really liked the term *wounded* because he looked at it in military terms. If someone from his platoon was wounded, then everyone was trained to go in to that battlefield and get him. He said that he sees his job as an intervention specialist in the school in the same way. He liked the idea that we were all in the business of saving wounded children, and he was to go get them and bring them back to the school for safety and healing.

Building Relationships

The previous chapter discussed how important relationships are for the wounded student, or any child. However, building relationships with a wounded child has its own set of skills and knowledge. Students that are wounded depend on relationships to build trust. Trust is established using grace, mercy, and forgiveness. Due to a wounded student's broken past, these terms help to allow some space for personal growth. These qualities are important in all relationships, but especially with wounded children.

Grace

The first part of building this relationship is grace—as I go around speaking, many people have asked, "Why use the term *grace*?" I believe the term certainly describes teachers and the way they think about their students. The (Merriam-Webster Online Dictionary, 2008) online definition describes grace as the quality or state of being considerate or thoughtful, or a disposition to or act or instance of kindness, courtesy, or clemency, or a temporary exemption (as stated in chapter 5). How many of us as teachers have had to give a student grace, as the defined above, to get them through a day?

If this is not true of our own lives, why should we not give it to the students in our schools? We may have to go out of our way or comfort zone in order to help a wounded student on a temporary basis. We want to make sure we do not help children develop negative behaviors or support dysfunctional actions. It is appropriate to give that temporary help and understanding because of a student's circumstances. You cannot let that student use you as a crutch permanently. If allowed, it could harm them in the long run. This is why specific programs that fit your community and school culture in order to address student behaviors are so important. During this time of exemption, students are learning and we are teaching a new way of handling behavior.

Mercy

Another term important to relationship building is *mercy.* Merriam-Webster (2008) online defines *mercy* as compassionate treatment of those in distress. Many of you can identify the students in your classroom who are in distress, but identifying and understanding how to address those students are entirely different issues. We had a student in our school who was abusing drugs and was headed down the wrong road. His life was in distress. He needed help before he continued to harm himself or possibly harm others. The school team of teachers and counselors developed a plan for him that also involved his parents from the start. The team allowed him time to be involved in a drug recovery plan from outside agencies that would include school as part of that process.

We told the student and his parents that when he completed the plan and had a clear drug screen, we would make him a speaker for our drug prevention program in the elementary school. The plan allowed for some grace and mercy and gave him a clear direction and time frame for his behavior and choices to change. No one in the plan accepted his behavior and gave no indication that it was all right to take his time to change this behavior. He needed to get put on a path of intervention for health reasons both mentally and physically. The young man completed his drug program after school and then received a clean drug screen. This young man became a role model for the other students in our schools for how to stop taking drugs and also assisted and encouraged others to follow him in his new leadership role. He had all the skills needed to be a leader; we had to make sure he channeled it for good.

Eventually, this young man's grades improved because his attendance and self-esteem improved. The goal was to meet the student where he was and take him to a place of achievement both in and out of the classroom. All of the credit goes to the individuals who where involved helping this student set a new course of hopes and dreams. The fact of supplying the proper resources at the front end and at the point of this student's wounds (drug use) was beneficial to recovery.

Some might argue that the schools should not deal with these issues and look at how much time it took to set up a program with the parents and local agencies. I would agree that this did take time and extra care. But it is better to deal with successful outcomes because we worked on the front end rather than deal with all the consequences on the back end. If this student kept going in the direction that everyone knew he was headed, we would have still spent that time invested with the student on the back end with the probation officers coming to our school and parents who would have to make sure that their son was in school.

Forgiving

Another term that I truly believe is critical for working with wounded students is to be *forgiving*. Forgiving means allowing room for error or weakness (Merriam-Webster Online Dictionary, 2008). How can we be effective teachers if we do not understand that our students are going to make mistakes, just as everyone makes mistakes? It is all part of the learning process. Forgiveness will allow us to accept our students for who they are and where they are today. A lack of forgiveness also makes everyone in the classroom and school feel heavy; it sets the school climate with the stale air of expected perfection and could get in the way of healthy relationships.

One day, before my daughter's first year of school, we were driving past the school grounds and she said to me, "Daddy, I don't want to go to school." I told her that I didn't understand, I thought she should be excited to go to school. She explained her fear to me, what if she didn't understand what they were saying? I said that when she first starts she may not understand but she will learn. The teachers are there to teach her about new things, and they will guide her to the answers so that she will grow into a good student. The most important part of the conversation was that I told her that she will always be learning new ideas and subjects from other people and she needed to be excited for those opportunities.

At the end of her second grade year she was not progressing academically as hoped. The teachers and school administrator laid out a plan for her success so that instead of making her feel like a failure, she was filled with promise and hope. She was only a little girl who needed some extra time to mature. They offered to have her repeat the second grade and met her at her emotional and academic needs. This was the best move for her at the time. Her fears about school that she first started out with could have happened. The school culture she was a part of said it is alright to need help and/or struggle with school. It does not have to be that way forever. My daughter learned to trust her teachers and understood that they where there for her benefit.

With the school's help she has matured since. Today, as an eighth-grade student, she is involved in many extracurricular activities and an A student. Her confidence was boosted at her early and formative years by her teachers and school. My wife and I will be forever grateful for their ability to be flexible and caring with our daughter. She also learned one of the most important lessons a person can: help others who are in need of you, and forgive them for mistakes in the past. Her teachers modeled it for her. My daughter also has goals to be a counselor at a summer camp in the area that helps other young children who are struggling at an early age with school or other issues such as esteem. Again, those school teachers set in motion a pattern in my daughter's life that says "It is noble to help those who are struggling."

I believe today teachers will always help their students when they understand the issues at hand. The problem is that today it is not always easy to understand all the issues our students are dealing with. Sometimes we struggle as much as our students to try to find the right solution to help them.

I have also seen the opposite of this with a few teachers who have had a difficult time with the concept. One teacher came to me one day frustrated and said, "These students are not ready to learn. They have too many things that get in their way." I agreed. This is why teaching is an art form that requires skill, training, practice, and patience. You must approach your day with the attitude that all students can achieve and that you have the professional training and performance that could determine the outcome of their success in the classroom.

During a seminar a veteran teacher of 32 years informed me, in front of everyone, that she believes I am putting too many unrealistic expectations on teachers. She said that you cannot make that big of an impact on every child you teach and that many new teachers will become frustrated with this concept and feel they are failing their students. I responded that I am speaking about wounded children, not because I believe every teacher has to have a dramatic influence on every student he or she comes into contact with; I am speaking on wounded children to properly identify the hard job that is in front of our teachers today, and to be sure we do not unknowingly do any additional harm to those entering our classrooms.

Personally, my goal is to help teachers today understand that some of these children are coming into their classes with hurts, scars, wounds, and trauma that some of us have not had to deal with in the past. In addition, like the title of the book states, we begin a new level of understanding that then leads us to proper training, and finally to reaching the academic needs for our students who are hurting. Through your understanding, you just may be the dramatic influence on a child's life.

The Importance of Professional Growth

When I speak to teachers throughout the country, I ask how many of the people there are completely satisfied with the school or school district they are associated with at this time or with the education system as a whole. Very few people raise their hand; they just keep their hand down and feel unhappy and powerless. Here is the good news: I am empowering you to teach, to take your new information and build on it to gain even more knowledge about all of your students, your community, and your profession. The field of education has changed more than any other profession in the past 30 years, including technology available such as the Internet, instant messaging, and endless television channels, along with the poverty, broken homes, and newly accepted norms.

When I made the comment at one conference that we are suspending 18,221 public school students a day from our public schools (Children's Defense Fund, 2008b), one teacher yelled out that we need to get rid of 18,221 more. Honestly, when I look back, I am not sure if that comment motivated me or saddened me.

Let me give a few more facts that I believe help us to see the need for change in our profession:

- Every 35 seconds a baby is born into poverty.
- Every minute a baby is born to a teen mother.
- Every 5 minutes a child is arrested for a drug offense.
- Every 9 minutes a child is arrested for violent crimes.
- Every 5 hours a child or teen commits suicide.
- Every 6 hours a child is killed by abuse and neglect (Children's Defense Fund, 2008a).

I could continue with these staggering statistics that should make anyone in our country stand up and take notice. One teacher told me that it is not our job to address these issues. I will agree that it may not be the job you signed up for, but I know it is the job we all believed in from the start. And I believe that teachers have the ability to make a difference. It just so happens that we signed up for the job that is going to test that in all of us. We all need to stand strong and faithful for that belief. Even though the outside influence in our culture demands our attention, the human condition and our most valuable treasure, our children, have not changed. Our students want to be safe, feel needed, and be connected with those around them. Those emotional needs and self-esteem issues were important to students 50 years ago and will still be important 50 years from today.

We need to develop programs that say we like you, we need you, and it is not the same without you: you have something to offer today and in the future. Let me bring the word out that most wounded children lack: Hope. I offer this information to you for your encouragement. Believe in a better tomorrow for all of your students. I appreciate and honor what you are doing.

I am doing it along with you, and I know you care about your customers more than any other profession out there.

"A recent survey by Optum Research, a Minnesota-based company that studies work-related health risks, found that 88% of teachers experience moderate to high levels of stress" (Crute, 2004, para. 4). When I read this, I realized that it obviously bothers us that we are not reaching our students. At every presentation I've given, someone has asked, "What about the wounded teachers?" We are hurting, too. Adding to the stress are the many expectations put on performance without the resources or training to obtain the ever increasing standards for all students. I do not believe educators have an issue with increased expectations; it is wondering how we meet those expectations in environments that can be less than desirable at times. I encourage you to apply the principles in this book toward your students and you will both see the benefits. The control battles will be over, and it will affect your school's culture. No one wants to go to a place where they feel they are not wanted or not making a difference. I believe that teachers are the difference makers if you only believe it and take action today. We need warriors who are ready to get into the race.

While training one summer with my wife to run some road races, I heard a good training technique. When you are out on the road and you start to get tired and want to quit, start speaking truth into your mind. You need to say to yourself, "I am strong and well trained." By repeating this truth to yourself you will have the strength to pull through. I do believe that teachers are strong and well trained. I ask you to start saying this along with me and fellow teachers. If you feel that you need to put in more training for a more difficult race or a new course ahead, put in time. Find the right personal or professional trainer to help make you a stronger teacher and team altogether. Think what this type of attitude would do for our students. We are their role models and if we are training hard, so will they.

Today, do not be a victim. Start being a beacon of hope for our wounded children. When I coached sports, I did not like the saying, "practice makes perfect." That just tells us that if you put in your time, then no matter what you do, you will improve. Nothing could be more wrong. I tell my athletes and students in the classroom and students who are trying to change their lives for the better, "perfect practice makes perfect." Practicing the correct behaviors and academic skills will make the marked improvements needed for our students. Sometimes we develop programs like detentions or suspensions that say put in your time but leave out the new behaviors the student needs to be practicing while there.

We can say that we have professional development days and continuing education or course work to keep our certifications current. This will not make it better if we are practicing the wrong things. Our professional development days should produce a result that asks, "How do we make every student welcome at our school and in our classrooms? How do we increase self-esteem in our students?" After these types of professional development days, watch your attendance soar. "Is every student leaving my classroom a better individual overall academically, behaviorally, emotionally, and morally in comparison to when they entered it 9 months ago?" It's all about the tough stuff.

Remember, you have practiced and studied new ways of thinking. If you find the old way works for you and you get results, then I encourage you to stay with that method. But, I believe that some "old school" methods work because they are based on ideas similar to those above but are just called something different. Maybe you don't like *grace* or *mercy* as terms, but I have heard of some people use words like *heart, compassion*, or *trust*. It all boils down to the same values.

Get the Parents Involved

To make sure we do not lose sight of the most valuable resource in reaching these wounded children, you must do all you can to develop programs for parents at an early age and then continue that relationship with the parents throughout the school years. Some parents will even make the comment that they feel they are wounded parents, or recognize they are dealing with their own problems. Still they appreciate people who are willing to help their child. Many of them do recognize that education can be their children's way to a new life. Many of the parents recognize how much different their lives may have been if they had completed school or furthered their education.

One elementary school developed a program to help students who where either at risk or wounded. As you read, keep in mind that at an earlier age, students may fall into the category of *at-risk* before wounds happen to them, but wounds can happen even at an early age. The program was designed for Grades 4-5 and lasted 10 weeks. The partners in the program were the parents, teachers, school counselors, and some outside support agencies. The program was designed to meet for 2 hours in the evening once a week for 10 weeks. The classes were divided for the students to meet with the group counselors while the parents met with the teachers. For the first hour each group discussed the areas where they could assist the student to become more successful during the school day. After 1 hour, the students and parents switched groups.

The parents were very appreciative that the school supplied these types of resources for their children early on. The students felt more connected to their school and teachers because of the extra time invested in them. And the teachers felt like they were providing intervention programs at an early age that are more specific to the children's needs, and they had support of the most influential part the children's lives: the parents. After the 2 hour program, a meal was provided for everyone so they had time to talk socially as well to develop relationships with each other. The program lasted from around 4:00–6:00. Those times can be adjusted to meet your parents' and school's schedules.

Key components to the program:

♦ involve parents early on;

♦ model student behavior;

♦ build self-esteem at an early age;

♦ students and parents feel better connected to the school; and

♦ deal with behaviors for academic success during nonacademic times.

The program was supported by a grant that the teachers and administrator acquired. The cost to operate was $7,500. The grant paid for outside support if requested as well as the meals or any activities provided for students such as field trips or supplies.

The Bottom Line

Earlier in the book, I said that teachers make a difference in their students' lives. I had a professor at Ashland University, Dr. Gregory Gerrick, who left the biggest impression on me about how to approach my career and the effect we can all have. He told the class one day that the organizational structure of public education is one of the slowest changing processes. We may not live to see the fundamental redesign of public education, but we can set that process into motion and we can have the satisfaction of knowing we are making a difference today and in the future. Thank you to Dr. Gerrick for modeling that change for our students and honoring the work and power that teachers have in our schools. You started my professional mission in motion on that evening class at Ashland University many years ago. You see, one teacher can make a difference in a student's life.

We have to understand that any child who is walking around with no hope is a wounded student. It is all about hope. What do most of us on the planet fear the most? To hear the words, "I am sorry. There is nothing we can do for you; there is no hope for you." What could be more devastating to the human spirit? Many of these students start life with this thought in their day-to-day lives. The wounded children in our schools are living day-to-day hoping the next day will bring the hope they are searching for. It is as though they are hoping for hope.

It can be our mission to restore this hope not only for their academic achievement but for the human race. I believe we can help wounded children develop new behaviors and new ways of thinking that can keep them from their destructive belief system, and keep from losing them to the ills of our throw-away society. These wounded students need us to use positive words of encouragement to help reach those wounds that need to be addressed. By developing the relationship of teacher and student, realizing that teachers are the second biggest influence in any student's life and that it only takes one teacher to turn a student's life around, we will start to change our education system.

I heard it said that never before in the history of our world are our children more in need of a hug, and never before in the history of our world are we less willing to hug them. We need to make sure that we do not abandon our children's emotional needs and then expect them to respond with successful outcomes.

Remember that we are all students and teachers at the same time. My years with wounded students have taught me about compassion, mercy, sadness, forgiveness, grace, and hope. I, in the end, found out that they were my greatest teachers.

Chapter 8 Key Points

- ♦ Building relationships helps establish trust.
- ♦ Three main relationship builders are grace, mercy, and forgiveness.
- ♦ Students need to feel safe, needed, and connected to be successful in school.
- ♦ Involve parents early on and keep them involved in your schools.
- ♦ Develop programs in elementary school for wounded children.
- ♦ Professional growth is needed in the area of emotional needs of wounded students.

From the Desk of Joe Hendershott

I hope that this book provides you with the understanding of why so many children today are hurting and lost. Through that understanding, together we can start the process of reaching their wounds so that they can be successful in school, in society, and in the rest of their lives. My passion is to start a new cycle in the lives of these children so that they will then pass it on for generations to come.

I ask that you use this book as an opportunity to take time and reflect on your profession or calling and realize the power that you possess as a teacher. A teacher is the biggest influence in a child's life outside the role of his or her parents. What an awesome responsibility we have been blessed with! This is a time to motivate and inspire one another in our mission as teachers. I have had the pleasure during my career to work with excellent school systems, administrators, teachers, therapists, counselors, and various staff members. During this time, I have seen professional people like you put their heart and soul into this calling of working with children. I am appreciative for all of your hard work and dedication that will benefit generations to come. I hope I have inspired you as much as you have inspired me to keep reaching out to offer freedom to hurting children.

My goal for you is that you become the voice for the wounded children in your professional and community settings. Let the journey of hope begin. Your students, to whom you have been given, are counting on you. I know they will make it with your understanding and grace.

~ Joe

References

Alliance for Excellent Education. (2006). *Saving futures, saving dollars: The impact of education on crime reduction and earnings.* Retrieved August 13, 2008, from http://all4ed.org/files/savingfutures.pdf

Alliance for Excellent Education. (n.d.-a). *About the crisis.* Retrieved February 6, 2008, from http://www.all4ed.org/about_the_crisis

Alliance for Excellent Education. (n.d.-b). *About the crisis, education in the states.* Retrieved August 16, 2008, from http://all4ed.org/about_the_crisis/schools/map

American Foundation for the Blind. (2008). *Helen Keller biography.* Retrieved August 13, 2008, from http://www.afb.org/asp?sectionID=&top12id=129

America's Second Harvest: The Nation's Food Bank Network. (2006). *Hunger and poverty statistics.* Retrieved August 16, 2008, from http: //www.secondharvest.org/learn_about_hunger/fact_sheet/poverty_stats.html

Bost, L. W (2008, June). *Helping students with disabilities graduate.* Retrieved October 14, 2008, from http://www.betterhigh-schools.org/docs/bost.ppt#739,4How Many Drop Out?

Brian, M. (1998). *Emphasis on teaching: What is good teaching?* Retrieved November 14, 2007, from http://www.bygpub.com/eot/eotl.htm

Children's Defense Fund. (2004). *Where America stands.* Retrieved June 16, 2007, from http://campaign.childrensdefense.org/data/america.aspx

Children's Defense Fund. (2008a, March). *Each day in America.* Retrieved April 2, 2008, from http: //www.childrensdefense.org/site/pageserver?pagename=research_national_data_each_day

Children's Defense Fund. (2008b, March). *Moments in America for children.* Retrieved April 2, 2008, from http://www

.childrensdefense.org/site/pageserver?pagename= research_national_data_moments

Cohn, A., & Carter, A. (2003). *Bullying: Facts for schools and parents.* Retrieved August 21, 2008, from http://naspoline.org/ resources/factsheets/bullying_fs.aspx

Crute, S. (2004). *Teacher stress: Stressed out.* Retrieved August 23, 2008, from http://www.nea.org/neatoday/0401/stressed .html

Dictionary.com. (n.d.) Retrieved August 16, 2008, from http:// www.dictionary.reference.com/browse/wounded

Douglas, F. (2006). Thinkexist.com. Retrieved October 12, 2008, from http://thinkexist.com/quotes/frederick_douglas/

Emerson, R. W. (2006). Thinkexist.com. Retrieved October 12, 2008, from http://thinkexist.com/quotation/the_secret_of_ education_lies_in_respecting_the/10710.html

Glasser, W. (2006). *Thinkexist.com.* Retrieved October 12, 2008, from http://thinkexist.com/quotes/like/effective-teaching- may-be-the-hardest-job-there/397307/

Hill, B. (2008). *Children and stress.* Retrieved January 21, 2008, from http://teachers.net/gazette/jan08/archive/

Merriam-Webster Online Dictionary. (2008). Retrieved August 14, 2008, from http://www.merriam_webster.com/ dictionary/grace

Orphan's Hope. (2008). *Our vision.* Retrieved October 13, 2008, from http://orphanshope.org/our_vision.html

Redenbach, S. (2004). *Self-esteem and emotional intelligence: The necessary ingredients for success* (Rev. ed.). Davis, CA: Esteem Seminar Programs and ESP Wise Publications.

Redenbach, S. (2004). *Self-esteem and emotional intelligence: The necessary ingredients for success* (Rev. ed.). Davis, CA: Esteem Seminars Programs and ESP Wise Publications.

Shaohannah's Hope. (2006). *Show hope: A movement to care for orphans.* Retrieved August 21, 2008, from http://members .shaohannahshope.org/site/pageserver?pagename= showhope_why

Silent Epidemic. (n.d.). *Ending the silent epidemic: The high school dropout crisis and its crisis.* Retrieved October 13, 2008, from http://www.silentepidemic.org/pdfs/take-away.pdf

St. Clair, J. (n.d) *What causes bullies?* Retrieved August 21, 2008, from http://www.byparents_forparents.com/causesbullies .html

Toppo, G. (2007, March 29). Study gives teachers barely passing grade in classroom. *USA Today.* Retrieved October 13, 2008, from http://www.usatoday.com/news/education/2007-03-29-teacher-study_N.htm

Yazzie-Mintz, E. (2006). *Voices of students on engagement: A report on the 2006 High School Survey of Student Engagement.* Retrieved October 12, 2008, from http://ceep.indiana.edu/ hssse/pdf/HSSSE_2006_Report.pdf